T0171503

SHEER GRACE

REFLECTIONS ON A LIFE

BLESSED BY THE GRACE OF GOD

Duain William Vierow

Trafford rev. 05/04/2011

 www.trafford.com

North America & international
toll-free: 1 888 232 4444 (USA & Canada)
phone: 250 383 6864 ✦ fax: 812 355 4082

Dedicated to Donna

who is the instrument of God's grace to me.

TABLE OF CONTENTS

INTRODUCTION

As I look back over seventy-six years, I find it extraordinary what God has done in my life, not through any virtue or extra effort on my part, but by sheer grace. It is like a dream, yet I know it was real, and I cannot help but be grateful and wonder why.

"Oh Lord, you are our Father,
We are the clay, you are the potter;
We are all the work of your hand." Isaiah 64:8

As an artist, I can relate to this Biblical metaphor. As the potter takes the raw material of clay and molds it into a form, so I too do believe that God works in our lives.

For a time I was an artist who delved into clay. I found the texture and elasticity exhilarating. Parkinson's would not allow me to continue, reminding me of the limitations we face in creating anything of beauty. But God does not have such limitations, except those we impose, in creating a work of lasting beauty. Even more, God the potter, keeps working, molding us as life progresses.

The trick is to be the kind of clay that has enough give to be molded according to the wishes of the potter. At times I'm sure I have been resistant. But God has been patient with me and shaped my life as I have gone along. I have always known I am in the tender care of His hands. When I have been humble enough to yield my will to His, He has made me an instrument of His grace. The beauty in the emerging work is a testimony to the potter's skill to create.

What follows is the story of one person's journey: an imperfect, dirty lump of clay on the Potter's table, there to find a full, meaningful life, touched with the grace of God.

May you be blessed as you read. I urge you to look behind and beyond the words to the flow of grace that I hope will be transparent.

Thanks to Betty Arnold, who worked on an earlier draft; to Frank Hutchinson for his comments and suggestions; and to Mary Lindskog for her editing.

PROLOGUE – HERITAGE

My parents, William Paul Otto Vierow and Louise Ottilia Wendel, were of German heritage. Both, however, led very different lives before they were married.

Father

My Father, Wilhelm (the German form of William) was born in a small village, Ganschendorf, in northeastern Germany on November 29, 1901. Wilhelm's grandparents were Heinrich and Caroline (Anders) Vierow. They were farmers with six children: four sons and two daughters. Henrich and Caroline first lived in Neu Sommersdorf, where they worked on a large government farm. They also lived in Toerpin (Caroline's home town), subsequently moving to Ganschendorf, where they worked on a large estate belonging to Baron Von Malzen before buying a small farm in Verchen.

Wilhelm spent his early years on that small farm in Verchen just meters from the Cormoron Sea, which was actually a large lake. The farm was situated within the confines of the village of Verchen.

Wilhelm was born out of wedlock. His mother, Matilda, and a local young man had an affair that resulted in the birth of my father. The man's name was Fritz Holtz. He would later marry my grandmother and they would have two more children, two girls, Herte and Ella.

Verchen was a conservative community, and this situation obviously presented a unique challenge to the family. My father was taken into his grandparents' (Henrich and Caroline) home and raised as their child, even taking their name (Vierow) in baptism at the local Lutheran Church. He apparently was well cared for and accepted by the community. He saw his mother and father, as well as his sisters, frequently as they lived close by. It has been my privilege to visit Verchen and family members in the area, including my Aunt Ella on three occasions, beginning in 1989. By the third visit "Tante" Ella had died. Through these visits I have been able to understand and appreciate my father's background and character.

In his later years my father would share a few stories of his early life: how he had older brothers (whom he also described as uncles) who served in the First World War; how he went to the local grade school and rang the church bell each day with his grandfather. There was no education available locally beyond eighth grade. It was decided that Wilhelm would attend a horticultural school in the nearby town. These classes focused on learning basic facts and skills for a vocation in horticulture. He worked at home on the farm, but it apparently became obvious that he did not have much future there despite the fact that he loved flowers and plants.

With several uncles living there and sharing a meager life style, it was clear he needed to seek his future elsewhere. So with this horticulture training and a depressed economic situation, Wilhelm left his home area to seek employment in one of Germany's growing cities. He was able to find a job as a gardener for a wealthy family in Hamburg. It was during this time that he met Carl Berg with whom he formed a lifelong friendship. By the time the early twenties came, Germany was suffering from the aftermath of the war. Wilhelm would later describe how he had hundreds of thousands of marks that would buy little, if anything, in the market. He searched for a better life that had promise.

With his newfound friend, Carl Berg, he decided to take advantage of a contact he had in the United States. An uncle (Ludwig) had immigrated with his parents and ended up in St. Paul, Minnesota.

Uncle Ludwig would provide Wilhelm's train fare from New York to St Paul should he decide to come. Living near Hamburg, a seaport from which many ships left for America, my father had undoubtedly heard about the promising new country and its openness to immigrants from Europe. With little hope of any quality of life where he was and feeling somewhat adventuresome at 22 years of age. He and his friend, Carl, decided to immigrate to the USA.

During a visit to his family in Verchen he told his sister Ella that he would return to see her (which was not to be). Then the two lads set off on a journey that would change their lives dramatically. On October 27, 1923, they boarded a ship (the Manchuria) full of immigrants in Hamburg bound for New York. They traveled "deck class," meaning they had access to the main deck and crowded sleeping quarters. They survived the two-week trip, undoubtedly welcoming the sight of the New York skyline and Statue of Liberty. They were admitted to Ellis Island for immigration procedures on November 11, 1923. Health exams, documentation and orientation took several days. The regimen was undoubtedly complicated by the fact that neither of these young men spoke English. No doubt they were filled with fear, but also with excitement, as they were about to venture into this new land.. Not knowing what the future would hold, it took a great deal of faith and courage to launch this journey of a lifetime.

Finally they were cleared for entry into the States and were placed on a ferry going to New York City. One last hurdle remained. They needed to show that they had 50 dollars before they would be admitted into the country. Not having such funds, they approached an obviously wealthy German man on the ferry, explaining their predicament. He was gracious enough to provide them with the 50 dollars with the understanding they would return it to him when they got off the ferry. They did so and set their feet on American soil in Manhattan. Soon after, they boarded the train bound for Minnesota. They had three dollars and some change between them with which they purchased food for the trip. The three-day journey across over half of the USA ended when they arrived at the old Union Station in St. Paul.

The young men made their way to a taxi, and in their heavy German accent told the driver they wanted to go to "Frank Strasse." Having difficulty understanding them, the driver drove about the city for some time before deciding it was futile to try further. But then, as I suspect was common during that time and circumstance, understanding the plight these two young men were in, he took them home with him to an apartment building. There was a German family in the building that, though it was late at night, was happy to receive them. The family provided food and moved their children out of a bed for the young lads to sleep in. The next day these kind neighbors told the driver where the two immigrants wanted to go, and he delivered them to Uncle Ludwig Vierow's residence on the east side of St. Paul.

In a short time, my father started working for Mrs. Joy, owner of a dairy farm just north of Silver Lake in North St. Paul. Being of German background herself, she was open to providing the opportunity to someone new and undoubtedly could use the help on a busy farm. William and other hired hands were provided a house and a small wage. Mrs. Joy apparently was impressed with young William, took him under her wing, and became his mentor in learning English and adjusting to a new world.

Grandparents

I did not know my grandparents on my father's side since they were in Germany. I remember my father receiving letters from Germany. After a long time (during WW II) he heard from them. The letter lay on the table while we had dinner. Mother could hardly contain herself. "Aren't you going to open it now?" "No," my father answered, (perhaps realizing that it likely contained some bad news and he did not want to be emotional at the table). "It has waited this long, a few more minutes will not make a difference." He was right, of course. The letter did contain bad news of the death of his mother, as well as others in the family. It was a sad evening in our home.

Maternal Grandfather Wendel

The only grandfather I ever knew, Henry J. Wendel, was also born in Germany, in Bavaria on September 15, 1869. He immigrated to the United States with his parents in 1879. He settled in Lakeland, Minnesota, with his parents, Michael Wendel and Louisa (Cover), both of whom came from Bavaria. Henry had a sister who died of epilepsy. Henry apparently was a versatile worker, holding jobs as a fish peddler, lumberman, and an installer of new railroad along the St. Croix River on the Minnesota side. He married Louise Lang on October 16, 1892 in Lake Elmo, Minnesota. About that time he also began working for Luger's Furniture Factory in North St. Paul.

A few stories about my grandfather will bring out the flavor of his personality and the time in which he lived. Shortly after his marriage, he and his new bride moved into their home in North St. Paul. The wooden floors were cold in the winter, and Henry had the offer of a large rug that could be his for the taking, but the rug was in Lakeland, some 20 miles away. Henry walked to Lakeland, picked up the rug, and carried it on his back all the way to North St. Paul.

He apparently had leadership qualities and worked hard. He was foreman on the railroad lines and also at Luger's. Once, when he was working on the railroad, he and the men were returning to base camp at the end of the day. He had to urinate, so he walked off the path. Returning and attempting to catch up with the group, he came to a fork in the trail and was startled by a local Indian man standing there with his rifle. At the time and under the circumstances, this was scary. However, no communication took place, and my grandfather returned safely. One of the ways my grandfather kept track of his railway crew was to row across the river to the Hudson Tavern and from there watch his crew through binoculars.

One of the tasks that he had while at Luger's was to take a team of horses to pick up lumber in Minneapolis or deliver furniture. Henry was a man who enjoyed his drink so he would stop along the way to imbibe a bit. Since the horses knew the way home, he would sleep in the back and let the horses take him safely home. Once, however, when it was raining heavily, he went to the back of the wagon and covered himself up with canvas. When Henry finally got his bearings, the team of horses had taken him to White Bear, five miles off the mark. That was the only time the horses ever lost their way.

Grandma seemed to rule the roost in the house, but Grandpa had a refuge in the basement of their home at 721 Helen Street, just across the road from the factory. There he sharpened blades of all sorts for local people. He had a workshop and spent considerable time there. Each year he would make elderberry, dandelion or grape wine, which would keep him through the year. He would enjoy this in his basement and occasionally offer a sip to visitors. They usually refused when they saw that the glass he offered probably hadn't been washed since he made the wine.

One impression of my grandfather that has remained with me all of my life was his faithful attendance at worship. He had a certain seat in the second pew on the left side of the church, that people knew was his spot. He was faithfully there each week.

Henry and Louisa celebrated their 60th wedding anniversary together in their home with family. Shortly thereafter, he became ill and died of cancer like all four of his adult children at a later time. One son died at an early age. Grandma Wendel died from heart problems and dementia soon after Grandpa.

Mother

My mother, Louise, was born on July 3,1912, the "baby" of the family. Other than a brief time in St. Paul, she never lived more than a mile from the home in which she grew up. She was more the "apple of the eye" of my grandfather than of my grandmother, as a special relationship was evident between them. She cared for him in the room next to mine, refusing to admit him to a hospital for months as he struggled with cancer. I recall how she would spend long hours caring for him, even though she also had a full time job. Painful as it was, it seemed to me a relief both for him and my mother.

Louise attended local schools and was well liked by teachers and classmates. It may have been a surprise when she left school in the tenth grade. This may have been due to the depression. For at least two years she worked cleaning homes for wealthy St. Paul families. At age 17 she began dating and was soon swept off her feet by "Bill," a handsome, sensitive, immigrant German nearly 11 years her elder.

Courtship and Early Married Life

"Bill" (William) studied English for several years before he and his friend Carl passed their tests and were approved to become citizens. Louise was still in high school when her friend Minnie invited her to attend the swearing in ceremony of her boyfriend, Carl Berg, and his friend Bill Vierow. Bill and Louise started dating. Their common Germanic background gave them a basis for developing a relationship. She was an attractive local girl and he a sensitive and caring older man. They were married when the country was deep into the depression on October 24, 1930, at Louise's family church, St. Mark's Lutheran Church, North St. Paul. Bill became a member and both remained there until their death.

About 1928 Bill began working for a well-known florist in St. Paul, Holm and Olson. Here he could take advantage of his horticulture background and his love for flowers. He quickly became a grower, working many different tasks, but also specializing in African Violets. It was difficult to travel from North St. Paul to the west side of St. Paul. They rented a home near Bill's work on Goodrich Avenue, where they lived for about five years. My sister Rita was born on October 15, 1932.

Parents Bill and Louise Vierow, sister Rita and me
as newborn in St. Paul, 1935

1. THE SHAPING OF A BOY

GROWING UP IN NORTH ST. PAUL, MINNESOTA

My Mother indicated that I seemed reluctant to come into the world. I was a month late by her account and was turning blue due to whatever causes babies to turn blue. I later thought it significant that I was birthed on the day assigned to the Conversion of St. Paul on the ecclesiastical calendar, January 25, 1935. St. Luke's Hospital was near to the home my parents were renting on the west end of St. Paul.

Baptism was on March 17 at St. Mark's Lutheran Church on West Seventh Street. My godmother was Louella Eckstrand, a neighbor and friend. She was a single woman who would later become governess for the children of the editor of the Washington Post newspaper in Washington D.C. Uncle Louis Wendel, my Godfather, lived close by and I saw him regularly during my formative years.

When I was two years old my parents, sister, and I moved from St. Paul to my mother's hometown, North St. Paul. Undoubtedly encouraged by my mother who, for other than those brief years in St. Paul had never lived more than a mile from the home where she was born on Helen Street. Dad was able to get a loan from Holm & Olson. I believe it was for $1,800 and was used to purchase a home on Sixth Avenue near the heart of town. The house was in need of modernization, but essentially sound and apparently a good buy.

1

Upstairs were three bedrooms. A kitchen was downstairs, with two equal-sized rooms used for dining and living rooms. The basement contained a cellar, with furnace, and space for storage and washing. The house was big enough for our family plus a few others who were with us a great deal of the time.

The barn had space for a car (though we only had a car for a short time) and included area for chickens, pigeons, rabbits, and a goat. There was also space for a chicken yard off to the side.

This house was my "home base" for most of my growing-up years. It had an acre or so of land, so there was plenty of space for gardening, playing, keeping pets, and even hiding.

One of my earliest memories was taking a bath on Saturday night in the kitchen. We had a single water tap in the kitchen and an old tin washtub that was filled with warm water heated on our stove. We took turns bathing, and I recall that it was a happy time. Our amenities were simple but adequate. We had an outhouse in the corner of the barn about a 30 yard walk from the house.

Early Recollections

We walked to school each day, a distance of a little over a half-mile with shortcuts that included crossing the railroad tracks. When I was in the first or second grade, I was caught in a storm with pounding rain. In the midst of the storm when I was fighting the elements and became disoriented, I was picked up by strong arms and cradled in the bosom of a young man who was a high school student. The arms unfolded when he deposited me at my schoolroom and disappeared. I never did know the name of that compassionate soul, but I was eternally grateful. This type of care was extended to us as children of the community as we grew up in North St. Paul.

Our play area included not only our land, but also vacant lots from our house down to the corner and across Charles Street, where we frequently had "pick-up" baseball games. The whole neighborhood stretched up the hill to Henry Street. and from Eighth Avenue to the area behind Fifth Avenue as well. We wandered rather freely through this area and were usually within earshot when it was time for supper or it got dark. Until I was nine or so, dark was the time to be in. This was due in part to the fact that there were several other growing children in the area. We had our "Sixth Avenue Gang" of boys that hung out together, especially in the summer months, creating our own activities. Sometimes when it was raining, we would play games like monopoly on our front porch, which often seemed to be the gathering place. It was a simpler time when townspeople trusted and encouraged one another and kept tabs on the community children. There was a pride in being part of the community and a sense of belonging, with an understanding of responsibility for the well being of its members. This town of about 3,000 souls, seemed to be an ideal community in which to grow up.

Much of our playtime developed around war games as our nation was in the battles of World War II. The only negative encounter was when an older homosexual boy on the fringes of the community infiltrated our group and tried to get us involved in his activities.

Building a "Chug"

One day we decided to build our own "chug," or go-cart. We lived on a fairly steep hill so it was quite a natural thing. My colleague in all sorts of ventures, Dick Proulx, had an old set of wagon wheels. We found a set of "buggy" wheels, a wooden apple box, and some rope. With a lot of enthusiasm and ingenuity, we set to work in our backyard, the scene of many such projects.

We fashioned a workable cart. The main body was an old piece of lumber that we cut to size. The axles were mounted onto two 2 x 4s and the box was fashioned into a fairly comfortable seat. A few well-placed nails on either side of the front piece and the rope was used as a steering device along with a bolt in the front so that the wheels could be turned. With a little oil, we were set!

3

Down the hill we shot, one pushing off, another driving. We picked up speed as we went. We went far beyond the corner of Sixth and Charles. We made it almost to the back of stores bordering on Seventh Street, the main drag in town. We knew we had a winner! During the coming days there were refinements to the design, but nothing major. We entered into the town go-cart race and placed respectfully. We learned a lot, and had a good time with this and other projects.

An Afternoon with Rich

On a warm summer afternoon my cousin, Rich, and I were at Grandma's playing in the yard. It had to be in the 1940s because we were still quite young, and my mother was working at Luger's factory where her father was foreman.

The two of us together conspired to see what mischievous act we could get into. In the kitchen were some of those forbidden matches that we had been told were "off limits." We snuck into the kitchen and grabbed a bunch, taking them back outside to the haystack. Wow, we lit one, then another. Oops! Soon the haystack was on fire. Then all hell broke loose. We called to grandma, who called the fire department. The fire siren was heard from the town center nearby, and within minutes the fire engine and members of the volunteer fire department arrived and doused what fire remained. It was exciting! But two little boys really got a scolding.

It is interesting to note that Rich's dad, my Uncle Louie, became fire chief later and had the job for many years.

Extended Household

Until I finished high school, it seemed like there were always additional people living in our home. Mother was very caring and wanted to help out those in need of a place to stay. It also helped out (at least most of the time) with the budget. It seems like there was always space for more and an extra plate or two at the table. My mother managed the household expenses, and somehow there seemed to be enough for everyone. Merle Newman was a welfare kid that stayed with us for about three years along with his two sisters for a year. Cousin Sally lived with us for a while, as well as her brother, Bud, when he came back from World War II. We also had classmates that needed a place to stay. Harry, Del, and Barb were with us. I usually shared a room with someone until I was in high school. I remember when I got my own room and my mother said I could paint it whatever color I wanted. It ended up being "fire chief red" from floor through ceiling.

Perhaps the most interesting character of all was my Uncle "Louie" (Ludwig). He was getting on in years, facing dementia. He always wore a pair of coveralls and loved to sit on the steps of the back porch. Perhaps the most distinguishable feature about him was his mustache. He had a certain cup for his coffee that had a special lip on it to keep out the mustache.

We kids were fascinated by his favorite summertime hobby -- catching flies with his hands. He was very patient as he sat still with hands opened until an unsuspecting fly came along. Then he would close his huge hands and trap the fly. When the fly was dead, he would reach into his pocket and take out a matchbox and put the fly inside. We counted 15 flies in that matchbox. Just how many days that took him, I did not know.

Dick Proulx

Dick Proulx and I were good buddies when I was in grade school. He was a bit older than I, so he reached junior high school age before I did and we went our separate ways, but for awhile we were together just about every day during the summer months. Others joined us in the neighborhood -- Ken, Ron, Stan and Del were all at one time a part of the "gang."

During my younger days we built a "shack" in a remote part of our land -- one that would be only for "members" and exclude girls. We dug out the lower part and placed a makeshift roof up about a foot from the tip so that we could look out and see if anyone was coming. One time we decided we were going to build a boat and sail, or rather push, our way across a swamp located near us. We built what we thought would be a seaworthy vessel out of old lumber and dragged it over to the swamp. Getting into the boat, we launched into the deep water only to watch it sink under our feet. We never did bother to rescue the boat and went on to more feasible projects. During the fall we had tomato fights or sometimes apple fights, though tomatoes were always softer and mushier when they hit. And in the winter, of course, we built forts and had snowball fights.

I remember going up to the Proulx home (it was, literally, up the hill, on the other side of the street) at breakfast time. Mrs. Proulx would always have the "Breakfast Club" on the radio, and I can still hear their jingle: "Good morning breakfast clubbers, good morning to ya, you woke up bright and early to a howdy do ye ... "

Radio was an important means of communication. I remember listening to Franklin Delano Roosevelt's address to the nation after Pearl Harbor. And we spent an exciting evening around the radio listening to the fight for the "heavy-weight championship of the world" between Joe Louis and Jack Dempsey.

Our main radio in the living room was large -- an old floor model that had the speaker down below and the switches and dial toward the top. When I became a teenager I listened to sports on the radio, particularly the games of the St. Paul Saints.

On Saturday afternoons the weekly children's matinee was at our local theatre, the Rialto. It cost 10 cents admission. A typical menu was a newsreel of national and world events, focusing on the war effort, cartoons (Donald Duck, Mickey Mouse, Popeye the Sailor) or short comedy (Three Stooges) topped off with a good cowboy movie (Hop-along Cassidy or The Lone Ranger). There was always a special matinee just before Christmas when Santa would appear and bring goodies for the children, followed by the screening of the film, "Father Knows Best."

The Town

North St. Paul was a quiet town of about 3,000 when I was growing up. We lived just a stones' throw from the town center. The main street (Seventh) crossed with Margaret Street in the center of town. When I was in high school we finally got a traffic light. We thought we had arrived in the big time. On both sides of Seventh Street were four bars, three grocery stores, two clothing stores, a barber, a drug store, a dime store (five and ten cent), a movie theatre, bowling alley, hardware store, and a couple of places for kids to hang out (one had a pool hall in the back). And there was Mac's hamburger shop, where for a few cents we could get the tastiest burger this side of St. Paul. There was a library, post office, and newspaper/printers.

Community events (other than church functions) were the annual Fourth of July parade, the school homecoming parade and the ice cream social at the lake. There was a Catholic grade school, but by the seventh grade almost all the kids in town went to the same public school. There was a move to consolidate schools when I reached high school.

Streetcar tracks ran through the center of town, transporting people to downtown St. Paul, a distance of about 10 miles.

Homesick

Early on I was taught the value of work and a job well done. I started odd jobs in North St. Paul. Those activities launched a varied job experience through seminary years. I cut lawn for a woman up at Silver Lake. Because we had a large vegetable garden, we would clean up various vegetables and place them in my red wagon. Then my sister and I would tour the neighborhood selling our goods. Like most kids, I also sold lemonade. We also had yard sales.

When I was nine years old we all decided we were going to make some money detasseling corn in Wisconsin. It was during the war so, lacking manpower, the farmer welcomed kids. One of our parents took four or five of us down to Prescott, Wisconsin, where a hundred or so kids gathered to work. We were housed in a large army barracks with

7

row after row of beds. I was the youngest of our group -- probably in the whole camp. We were up at the crack of dawn and out in the fields early, with a break for a sack lunch. I think we earned something like ten cents an hour. The first week was exhausting, but manageable. Sunday we had off, and therein was a problem. Some of the parents of kids in our group knew Sunday was free for us so they piled into a car and came down to visit their sons. When they left, a huge case of homesickness set in. I complained of stomach troubles the next day, and was unable to work. The next day the director of the camp had business to attend to in Hastings across the river. He took me along and I remember going across the historic circular wooden bridge.

By the next day I think he thought he had enough of babysitting and took me down to the train station late in the afternoon and put me on a train headed for St. Paul. This was an adventure for a nine-year-old who hardly knew of any life beyond North St. Paul. But I had been to St. Paul several times and knew where to catch the streetcar to North St. Paul. After boarding, I sat in the first seat I saw and got chewed out by the conductor for sitting in his seat. When I arrived at the old Union Station in St. Paul (the same station my father had used in 1923), it was getting dark. I trudged with my suitcase several blocks over to Seventh Street where I knew I could get a streetcar. By the time I got off in North St. Paul, it was after 10 o'clock. Bag in hand, I walked up the hill to my home and pounded on the door to awaken my parents. They did not know what had happened or that I was coming. I was happy to be home. That was the only time in all my wanderings I experienced homesickness.

Caddying

At age nine I also decided to follow some neighbor kids to the Jewish golf course, Hillcrest Country Club, on the edge of St. Paul. We went by the first street car about 6:30 a.m. After getting approval from the caddy master, we put our names on the list of caddies and waited for a golfer to show up. There were "A" and "B" caddies. Of course I started out as a "B" caddy and had lots to learn. Aside from the practical jokes that they played on young beginners, I enjoyed being out of doors and with the guys. Caddying was something you could do part-time between other things. As the years went on, I continued to caddy occasionally until I was working full time in the summer months.

Mondays was designated as "caddy's day" when we got to play free. Dad and I went down to St.. Paul to an antique shop where I purchased an old wooden handled mashie and putter. I took them out to the course the next Monday with some balls I had found in the rough and hacked my way around all 18 holes. My life-long enjoyment of golf began. I am grateful for what caddying taught me about the game, rules, and expected conduct.

Ruffenacht's Farm

On a free day Dick Proulx, myself, and whoever else would join us would venture out.

After we crossed the road separating Ramsey from Washington County, we were soon in the land of Ruffenacht's Farm. Ruffenacht's, a dairy farm about five miles away, was the place to go as things were always happening there. It had 500 acres of friendly land, an extended learning experience for any young boy on a free day. We followed fences and other natural signs through the woods until we saw the farm buildings in the distance. The massive barn loomed large on the horizon. A high school student, Warren, was a helper on the farm. Mr. Ruffenacht was of German descent and a friend of my father's.

We used to spend time in their huge haymow, but the first order of business was checking out the projects Warren was doing. I recall he was out plowing one day, and I happened to be there when he finished. He asked whether I would like to ride the huge Belgian horse that was part of a pair they had. Wow, what a treat! I remember riding the huge back of that gentle horse, hanging on for dear life.

The Ruffenachts were understanding and knew our parents. But on at least one occasion they went above and beyond the call of expected caring. Several of us boys had decided we were going to "rough it" in

9

the woods at the farm. We backpacked our gear out to a green pasture several hundred yards from the farm. We were going to live off the land and so brought very little food. We were going to fish and catch game, etc. Game was nonexistent, at least with our skills and equipment, and fishing was a bust. We survived for several days by sliding around in a nearby pond catching frogs and frying legs. About the fourth day Mrs. Ruffenacht got wind of our plight and had us all in the house for a very welcome home cooked meal. It sure tasted good.

3M Tape Dump

In the vicinity of the Ruffenacht farm was the 3M Tape dump. This was in the '40s before regulations on disposal and toxic waste. Smoke emanating from the dump gave us a clue that there had been a recent visit by one of their delivery trucks. When we came up to the dump, protected only by a makeshift wooden fence (the kind that was used on the roads to keep the snow from drifting), we looked for rolls of tape (there were all sorts) that were not burned. We usually went home with a stick over our shoulder adorned by rolls of tape we had managed to salvage. We got some good use out of "throw away" tape, much of which had minor flaws in it. We used it creatively in repairing all sorts of gadgets and for wrapping gifts.

Chores Around Home

With both parents working there was a certain amount of work that needed to be done around the home. Dad left on the early streetcar at 6:30 a.m. for work and Mom was usually gone from 7:30 a.m. to 5 or 5:30 p.m. Besides things like doing the dishes, there were the pigeons to feed, coup to clean; caring for chickens, rabbits, a goat, a dog and cats. All needed care. Plus I had to stoke the furnace as soon as I got home. Basic tasks were done in a matter of less than an hour, but it was during the summer months that we pitched in with more substantial chores.

For it was during the summer months that our huge garden needed tending. Rows of beans, lettuce, carrots, peas, tomatoes, cucumbers, melons and squash needed attention. In addition there were several berry bushes, strawberries and trees that needed tending. There was plenty of time in the summer, so these were done early in the day.

At least once during the growing season, my sister and I would get out the red wagon and load it up with fresh vegetables and peddle them around the neighborhood. This was a pleasant task and seemed to make our neighbors happy; it also brought in a little income.

Discipline was part of our lives as children. I was expected to honor and obey our elders and to act in a way that would be appropriate. There was, of course, a certain leeway allowed, but I learned that broad diversion was not tolerated. When I didn't do the "chores" as told, I heard about it when Mother got home. If I hadn't peeled the potatoes for supper, I heard about it. "Wait 'til your father gets home" was the ultimate threat.

When Dad came home and he was angry, he took me down to the basement and paddled my behind. This didn't happen very often, but when it did, I'm sure it hurt Dad as much as me (though I did not think so at the time). To discipline me at the dinner table, he would pull my right ear. We used to kid that my right ear was bigger because it was pulled so often.

This stopped of course when I got into junior high school. I became active in all sorts of sports and had practice after school. I became bigger than my dad, but I was still expected to do "chores."

Christmas Magic

I will never forget one Christmas Eve. It was the kind of night from a picture post card. It was a magical evening. The temperature was mild and there was a light snow falling. We had already had some snow so everything was covered with a clean white sheet.

It was around 10 p.m., and we were walking (since we had no car) to church to attend the midnight service. We had spent the evening together as a family. I was probably about 10 or 11 years old. We arrived at church early. We waited for Pastor Rees to scurry across the street to the old church. He had celebrated the evening with his family, including two daughters, Marthetta and Janey, who were ahead of me in school. He realized he was a bit late and still had the candles to light for the candlelight service and asked if I would help.

As I went around the church lighting each candle, the evening took on a magical quality as worshippers arrived. Our family sat quietly as the story of Christmas, the Christ child born in Bethlehem to the Virgin Mary, was read again. "For unto us a child is given, unto us a son is born . . . and his name shall be called Wonderful Counselor, Mighty God, Prince of Peace."

War

As the U.S. entered the fray of global war, it affected our community and our family. Young men from the community had gone to serve their country. A flag hanging in a window on Eighth Avenue just a block and a half away had three gold stars on it indicating that three sons had died in battle. The "Greatest Generation," as Tom Brokaw would later describe it, was providing a mighty force for good at home and abroad. Loyalty to country, sacrifice for the common good, serving where there was a need, having a sense of personal responsibility, and commitment to the truth were characteristics of this generation. My older cousins all served in the military. One of them, "Bud" Brandt, would receive a purple heart for his bravery in France, where he lay on the battlefield wounded for eight hours before help came.

Dad, 40 years old and the head of a household, was exempt from military service. Due to a shortage of men in the work force and recognizing that the last child was in school and undoubtedly needing additional funds, Mom decided to work with her dad, the foreman at Luger's Furniture factory. It was difficult labor lifting tabletops and other wood. Mom needed more help from us children to make the household operate. She became frustrated at times, understandably so, and lashed out at my sister and me. She would work much of the rest of her life, but fortunately in less physically demanding and more fulfilling work.

We always knew we were of German descent. We learned certain words and customs, usually around the table at night, which was the time we were all together. My father spoke with a German accent his entire life.

One negative incident sticks in my mind. My father and a neighbor a few blocks away were both of German descent. When they got together, they would speak German. One day my father was working in the garden when his friend came down the street. They conversed in German loudly enough for passersby to hear. They were chastised for speaking in German and called "krauts." Perhaps there was a question of their loyalty to the USA because of this. Surely the anti-German sentiment was strong during the war years. Dad, of course, was a loyal American but he also did not want to "rock the boat." We were more cautious in speaking the words we knew, and I regret very much that Dad did not teach us German, as it certainly would have been helpful to me in later life.

Like other families, we participated in food rationing of staples such as flour and sugar and generally tried to conserve. We saved old tubes of toothpaste, collected as much as we could of aluminum foil, wrapping it into a ball (we had contests for the largest ball), and anything else that was needed in the war effort. One of the items that we heard was needed was milkweed silk for parachutes. We scoured the countryside for milkweed, collecting dozens of gunnysacks full. Just as we were about to bring them in, the authorities indicated that it was no longer needed. (That was toward the end of the war.) A friend's dad, however, was building a house and purchased the filled gunny sacks from us for insulation.

Fortunately, we had extra food available because we kept a number of animals. I recall some nights eating plain rice with cinnamon on top. We had several chickens, rabbits and pigeons. I butchered these animals, sometimes, when we were in need of protein. Still, I did not feel deprived in any way growing up. We were adequately clothed and fed, sometimes I'm sure at great sacrifice by our parents.

As the war drew to a close, it was clear that our relatives in Eastern Germany were having a rough time. Though we did not have a lot, we certainly had more than they. A spirit of cooperation and help prevailed. The Marshall Plan and other programs were started to help rebuild Europe.

It was during this time that we developed s plan to do what we could to help. I remember my parents collecting clothing and various foods (sugar, flower and coffee were especially welcome). My parents spent much time packing parcels. My job was to take out my red wagon, load the parcels on it after school and make a trip to the local post office. My parents had limited resources, so I was instructed as to the order of parcels, which should go first and which saved for next month when funds were available. Used shoes, boots, hats, scarves coats of all sizes, pants and dresses were packed with prayers that they might reach the family.

We received letters of gratitude from our family. I did not realize the degree of help until I visited East Germany back in 1987 (before the Berlin Wall came down and Germany was reunited). During our time with the family, we were told long stories of how those parcels had sustained them through a most difficult period. The connection across the miles was bridged in this act of caring and kindness from my parents. My first cousin in East Germany said that they looked forward to receiving the parcels with great anticipation. It turned out that they were the best dressed kids in school, because the rest of the students had only what was available locally. They shared with pride that their American relatives thought so much of them that they wanted to help.

Tears came to the eyes of my Aunt Ella and the three first cousins that I met for the first time. Hearing the story and the impact that it had made us teary eyed also. We were all filled with gratitude for the opportunity that presented itself long ago.

Family Gatherings

There were two places that the family would gather: the kitchen table for meals and all sorts of crafts and activities and around the piano in the dining room. A baby grand piano was the one extravagance my Mother had. She had purchased it when she was working at house cleaning prior to her marriage. Mom enjoyed playing the piano and occasionally would launch out in her rendition of "Falling Waters." As the years progressed, she yielded to my sister, Rita, who was quite an accomplished player and took lessons from one of the sisters at the Catholic School.

When I was growing up, especially in the 1940s, Rita and I, plus others who stayed with us, would gather around the piano and sing, mostly popular tunes of the day. We knew all the war tunes and had quite a repertoire of show and hit tunes, hymns and carols. Dad did not sing, but enjoyed listening. Mom did not sing well, but occasionally joined in. It was a time for bonding. Many an hour was spent singing around the piano with friends.

Games

During the summer months we played various games. Some were table games like monopoly (that could go on for days), but at other times we would want something more active, especially in the evening. Then we would divide up into teams and play "Capture the Flag." One team would take the flag, hide it, and then defend against the other team that was searching for it. Any person on the offensive team that was tagged by a defensive player would be declared dead. The game concluded when all the offensive team players were "dead" or the flag was captured.

With 10 or 12 players we would use all of our land plus the vacant lot on the corner. Once, when I was close to getting the flag and running toward it, an opposing player spotted me and came after me. In trying to avoid him, I ran smack into a tree! I was shaken up and had a gash above my right eye, requiring stitches. But it sure was fun!

Dad

Dad never made a good wage. His eighth grade education in Germany and consequent attendance at gardening school was admirable for his time and place, but it relegated him to a work he loved and a wage that he accepted. He worked long hours in addition to the more than an hour's streetcar ride to and from work, which cut into his time at home.

Dad found his calling in plants – in caring, nurturing, planting, planning and designing, using those marvelous expressions of God's created order, flowers and foliage, to bring delight, happiness, and hope to many. It was common for someone visiting our flower gardens (as many did) to go home with a freshly cut bouquet of flowers.

He remained humble throughout his life, attempting to live within the basic value system he was given: work hard, don't think too highly of yourself, remember your roots, value the family, be honest, help others, and be a faithful Christian. He often reminded me of Jesus' statement in the Sermon on the Mount: "Blessed are the meek, for they shall inherit the earth."

I most remember him in the garden at night watering the plants. Being close to nature, there was calmness about him. He was soft spoken and usually didn't enter into conversation easily. He was most at home in his garden, enjoying each new bud and taking in the seasons. He was generous with his flowers. The women in his life always received a corsage on special days.

I wondered if he really loved me. He didn't tell me and a minor crisis in my life made a difference. I was undergoing treatment for stuttering. The small Asian woman working with me was very understanding. She asked me, "Does your father love you?" I could not answer her. It was soon after that Dad took me on a camping outing over a weekend. Bud, my cousin and wounded hero from the war, was staying with us and dropped us off (tent and all) near the city dump at Cottage Grove about twenty miles from home. He picked us up two days later.

We spent the first minutes frantically pitching the tent as raindrops fell. When the rain let up, we went for a walk, found an old schoolhouse, and pumped water from a well. We didn't do much except spend time together, and I still have a large knife that Dad carved for me and placed the date on the handle. It's amazing that the stuttering stopped and I knew that Dad loved me.

Working with Dad

We didn't have much money because my father's work was low on the pay scale. But it was good, steady work that my father enjoyed and was good at, so we made do with the lower income. One of the ways we compensated for lack of income was that I joined the work force when opportunity came. When I was eleven or twelve years old, the same place where my father worked, Holm and Olson Florists in St. Paul, hired two young boys to help with the tagging, washing and carting of plants from the greenhouse to the place for decoration during the busy seasons of Christmas and Easter. (This was an intense period of two to three weeks twice a year when we worked long hours to deal with the rush of orders during the "busy" season.)

The pay was 35 cents an hour. I enjoyed working with Stan Hampel, the manager, and other workers. But the real joy was working with my Dad and seeing the respect others had for him. We often got home about 10 P.M., but it was temporary work during the time of break from school, and they brought in a delicious meal when we worked late.

I worked there for several years and graduated to decorator when I helped the ladies with decorating pots. I also worked there one summer filling in for those who went on vacation. Eventually my salary went up. It was a good experience.

Mom

Mom was definitely the driver in the family. She was the one who was socially active, involved in community affairs and known in town. She had drive as she worked full time, was a leader in 4H for over 20 years, was a Sunday School teacher, and active in village life. She wanted her family to be well thought of and tried to motivate us kids to excel.

She was a member of a number of community organizations like the Eastern Star and Women's Auxiliary. She served on the town's committees and supported events. As we were growing up, our home was always filled with other kids and they were encouraged to participate in projects of various kinds.

Mom would organize the making of things that could be used as gifts for people at Christmas or other times of the year, often utilizing pieces of lumber from Luger's factory. She enjoyed parties with friends and the couples' card club.

Family was very important to her and she was giving of herself beyond reason, often helping persons in need. She was a living example of a Good Samaritan. I felt supported by her especially regarding the decisions I made.

Mom and my sister developed a confrontational relationship. Rita was definitely the rebellious type, and there were some tough years. I sometimes got caught in the middle of an argument, but generally I stayed out of it. "Toots" (an endearing name that I use for my sister) and I have gotten along well. She was very supportive of me while in school. She had six kids, ended up living next to my parents for years, moved away for twenty, and is now back in Minnesota.

Summertime

The place to be during the warm summertime was the beach at Silver Lake, a mile's distance, which we usually covered by bike. We also did some fishing there, mainly bullheads. The small beach on the corner of the lake had a raft out in the deep and a lifeguard on duty. We learned to swim by trial and error. The big kids congregated around the raft. I remember the day I learned how to make it out to the raft. The big kids were out there, and I was all alone in the shallow area. I decided that I would try to go out to the raft. Getting about half way, someone spotting me from the raft – "Look, Sonny's coming." They cheered me on as I paddled to reach the raft. It was a good feeling, and I was never alone in the shallow water again.

By the time I became a teenager, however, it was time to work. I did all sorts of jobs: cut grass, worked at the greenhouse and State Fairgrounds, washed cars, and re-stuccoed houses. On the stucco jobs, I worked with a couple of notorious characters. At least one of them had been in and out of jail and led a pretty free life. Stuccoing houses, especially several stories high, was hard work. Once the ladder came out from under me, and I had a bad case of skinned arms, but I learned how to handle ladders and more than a little bit about life as others lived it. It was undoubtedly during this time that I decided that I wanted to pursue a vocation in life where one could work to accomplish something meaningful for society.

Winter Snow

When you live in Minnesota you had better enjoy getting out during the winter. For us, that meant skiing. At that time there was not a distinction between downhill and cross-country. There was just skiing, so when a relatively nice day came along and I was free from school during the winter, I would lock into boots that were harnessed onto heavyweight skis. I had two poles that we used to maneuver and off we would go across the countryside. With my buddies, I would head out to the woods toward Ruffenacht's farm.

There is nothing quite like gliding over fresh, deep, powdery snow. The skis I used were fairly broad with some spring in them. I became adept at crossing through barbed wire fences and moving through wooded areas. It would take us a good hour to reach an area where we built a small jump, a platform about 18 inches to 2 feet off the slope of the hill that we would use to test our skill. We would spend several hours there blazing new trails and jumping before heading for home again.

Years later, when I was up at the farm in North Branch during winter, I would hook onto the back of the car with about 100 feet of rope. I would travel down the county road at a pretty good clip with Harvey Schmidt, local friend and farmer, driving.

Later in life I still enjoyed cross-country skiing with my son, once on the University of Minnesota Golf Course when the wind chill was minus 90 degrees. Needless to say, we did not stay out very long.

Pets

We enjoyed many pets at home. Our dog, Shep, joined the family when I was baby and died when I was 16. He was truly a loyal companion. We always had one or more cats. My favorite pet, however, was Jenny. Like many a kid I wanted a pony and started saving funds to buy one. My parents, in their wisdom, decided an affordable route was to get a goat. We had $2.50 in hand when Dad and walked to the nearby goat farm. We looked at several goats, but could not afford them. Finally, seeing my aspirations, the farmer decided that a baby goat could go for that price. As soon as I saw the goat, it was love at first sight.

I carried her home in my arms, and "Jenny" and I became best friends. We started out by feeding her with a baby bottle. I spent much time with her and she followed me wherever I went, including my frequent shopping trips to the grocery store. Everyone knew where I was because the goat was waiting outside for me.

Perhaps the story that best describes our relationship took place one summer. I was ill with pneumonia. I had not seen Jenny for many days, and she was lonesome. The superintendent of schools, W. W. Richardson, paid a visit and was talking to my mother downstairs. The front door was open, and Jenny saw her chance! Feeling lonesome, Jenny took one look at that open door and scooted up the stairs to find me. I awoke from sleep with Jenny licking my face. I don't know who was happier. It was sad when we had to take Jenny to a farm for retirement.

Blessed in Freedom

I have always been grateful for the freedoms I had when growing up. While both parents were somewhat protective, I grew up in a caring community, which afforded me opportunities that many did not have. It was safe and strong in its commitment to nation and family. St. Mark's Church provided me with good basic Christian nurture. I had a high respect for my teachers and our Pastor Rees.

My early years were blessed in many ways. Like the potter shaping the clay into an instrument of service, I was being molded by the Master Potter.

My confirmation class at St. Mark's Lutheran Church

2. THE SHAPING OF A YOUNG MAN

NORTH HIGH POLARS

All 13 grades, kindergarten through twelfth grade, were at the same school. There was a handful of us who attended all the grades together. The North St. Paul School District was growing, however. Two elementary schools were added and then the entire "old" building was occupied by the high school.

When I graduated, we were the last of the small classes with just 71 students. The year following, there was about 150 and the following classes were larger still. There was an explosion of children in suburbia, but I had the benefit of being from a small class. In fact, I had some of the same teachers my sister and mother had.

It was Mrs. Anderson, my seventh grade teacher, who first recognized my artistic talent. Her encouragement was an inspiration.

Sports

I had played touch football and shot baskets at the hoop attached to the barn. We spent many an hour playing pick-up games in the backyard. Hal Norgaard, the physical education teacher and basketball coach, worked with us.

High School 1953

I was good enough in high school basketball to make the team, but not good enough to get significant playing time. Our home games were in the old gym that had bleachers along one side. There was a stage on one end and the other side had just enough space for the teams to sit. I sat at the far end of the line, to get away from the abuse of Coach Hal Norgaard's voice. "Veerrow, get the lead out!" I was not motivated to perform well for this guy. He did however coach some good teams and served the community well as a Lion's Club leader and county commissioner. When we were ahead by 15 to 20 points and there were about three minutes left in the ball game, Norgaard would take out the good players and substitute those who were at the end of the bench. Once I scored eight points in less than three minutes, the high of my basketball career. Perhaps it was Norgaard's shouting that turned me off. Still, we got to go to all the games free, and there was the ride on the bus to distant games with the cheerleaders. At any rate, I turned to football and golf as my sports.

Golf interested me from the days when I caddied at Hillcrest. Arnie Bauer was our coach. We played several matches around the area, but the big tournament was the suburban district meeting, an outing that I blew my senior year by hitting three balls in a row out of bounds.

Football

I was center on the junior high football team. I soon graduated to the varsity team as a sub. We practiced on the "dust bowl" which was also used for other sports, and by the time we got to football it was pretty much a dirt track. Football practice in August, before school started, was always grueling, and I remember well coming home from practice with all sorts of aches and pains, so by the time the "season" rolled around, we were in good condition. We played in the "Little Six" league, plus a couple of extra games. White Bear Lake always seemed to be a big rival.

The position of center was crucial to the team, and I was torn between working at the State Fair and practicing football my sophomore year. I chose the State Fair and lost the job of playing first-string center to Del Mottaz, a friend who did a great job. By my junior year I was the first string center again, and Del moved on to tackle. Back in those days centering was key as the ball had to go to all the backfield. I especially gave a wide lead to Denny Tito, our all-star tailback. The last year we played on a brand new ball field with bright lights and lots of bleachers.

Sid Shoegren was football coach my freshman year. Win Arns took over during my sophomore year. Felix Crepeau took over for the rest of my senior high years. He had a good rapport with the team. Not above playing a practical joke on one of us, he taught us the finer points of the game, like how to throw a cross-body block on the opposing end. This I did with great delight as I pulled from the center of the line and surprised the end who was a sitting duck for our reverse play. Being in the center of the line meant that I got the huddle going, and when I got over the ball I accessed the opposition. At the proper time, of course, the play started with me centering the ball. I went out for college football but had to withdraw because I needed money for my education.

When I was a freshman, in football I was on the second team and so got to play scrimmage during practice. Back in those days, this meant that I played linebacker on defense. I recall the big linemen coming at me, but one play stands out. Bill Sandberg, who was in my sister's class and later was mayor of the town for much of his life, was the first-string fullback and came charging over tackle. I met him at the line, threw myself in his direction and held on for dear life.

"Now, that's the way to tackle," shouted Sid Shoegren, the coach.

"Wow," I thought. "That's so different from Hal Norgaard's harsh words."

Friday nights there was a home game followed by a dance. Back in those days we did the "slow dance" which was much more intimate. Boogie-woogie was just coming into vogue.

Class of '53

We had a memorable class, with a variety of characters, students of promise, movers and shakers, class clowns, jocks, cheerleaders, and nerds. It was amazing that in a class our size there was such diversity. This made for an interesting mixture of personalities. In our older years we have had a class luncheon once a month at Gulden's Restaurant. Henri Knoll and Carol Dehen, two great communicators, coordinate this. Here, those who stayed close to home get together and anyone from out of town who happens to be around drops in. We are spread far and wide. Stan Stephens is an entrepreneur in Alaska; Harry "Wirk" Wirkkunen, the drawer of caricatures, is in Nevada. Some of us have retired in Florida or Arizona. Carmen Michael, who sold airplanes to Arab chiefs, is in California. I was the one who wandered farthest from home to the other side of the globe. Most of them have distinguished themselves.

High School Teachers

In addition to my coaches mentioned, I was blessed with some teachers who really believed in what they were doing and in the kids they were teaching. Doris Sweet was our social studies teacher and counselor. In my final interview with her, she said that I was in the top half of the class in grades, but in the upper quadrant in ability. Inadvertently, she handed me a paper on which was printed my IQ, then came back and said, "Oops, wrong page." I did not let on that I had seen it, but it told me that I was definite college material and had the smarts to make it. It gave me confidence.

Win Arns, Arnie Bauer and Gavin were all coaches who had me on their teams. Miss Larson was young and full of energy as our speech teacher. Mrs. Walters was a knock out, but not too effective as a teacher. The two teachers that I perhaps related to the best were Palmer Rauk (music) and Dick Scott (art). There were three of us (Herb Ketchem and Harry Wirkkunen) who got straight A's in art. Herb became an accomplished architect (designed the second phase of the Twin Cities airport). Harry was the caricature drawer in our class, went on the "U" (University of Minnesota) and ended up in Reno drawing sketches of people in Vegas, on cruise ships, at conventions and such places.

Dick Scott had arranged for a visit to his alma mater, Hamline University in St. Paul. I was offered a grant-in-aid (I recall that it was $800 per year, enough to cover tuition), and I enrolled there because I could live at home and save money that way. Dick Scott was easy to talk to and had an artistic flare. I recall doing a collage that had a feather in it. He suggested that a skimpy clad girl underneath the feather would add a quality of interest to it, so I put it in. These pieces were displayed on the board. The next day he told me that he had removed my work because L. C. Malo, the Principal, had told him to. I was editor of the "Polaris," the school yearbook, my senior year with Scott as our advisor.

Palmer Rauk was a member of our church where he directed the senior choir, which I was a part of all through my high school and college years. At school he was the music teacher, both choral and instrumental. He was enthusiastic, his one eye sharp as can be. He and Margaret, his wife, were a true example of a loving partnership. Mr. Rauk was the director of the choir (I was president and my sole duty was to help him with the selection of music), the Boys' Glee Club (won top honors in the state my senior year), as well as other choral groups. He was also director of the band (I played the tuba). I really enjoyed time spent on music.

Eleven of us were in the National Honor Society.

High School Cars

When I was sixteen and had worked that summer, I purchased my first car, a 1935 Pontiac Coupe, for $50. This also helped my mother, as I took her to get groceries, etc. It had running boards, so kids could hang on (which was illegal) in addition to the three that were inside. I would pull into the local gas station and get 25 cents worth of gas which lasted a couple of days. With wheels I was able to get to school and events a lot easier and take girls out.

The second car I had was a 1941 Black Ford fastback. My sister's boyfriend from St. Paul was a mechanic and bought the car (with the body in good shape). He was willing to work on rebuilding an engine, and I would have a going machine. It had skirts on the rear wheels, and I rigged up a bird with plastic wings that would light up on the front of the hood. Wow, it was really the cat's meow!

There are several incidents that indicate what a risk taker I was and how God was watching over me. Cruising over in Wisconsin, my old friend, Dick Proulx, and I were leaving the same function at the same time. Now, Dick was out of high school and had a Cadillac, sleek and black. I pulled up next to him at a stop sign. He gunned his engine as if to say, "Don't mess with a Cadillac." I responded by gunning my engine and we were off! I had a stick shift but kept up to him down the highway; I pulled out at 85 miles per hour because I had a big bulge in my rear tire (I could not afford a new set of tires).

Another time, traveling near the Bucher cabin over in Wisconsin, we found ourselves on country roads that were like roller coasters. The faster we went, the more thrilling the ride. We came flying over this hill and there was a huge bolder in the middle of the road! If I swerved, I would surely go off the road. I aimed straight for the boulder, and we went right over it. Now the car had quite a bit of clearance, but not enough for that boulder. Apparently the car had enough bounce in it from the speed that we sailed right over it, or was it that there was divine intervention?

Early one evening my sister, her boy friend, and I went out to Lake McCaren. My sister had to stop at a girl friend's house, so the two of us jumped in the lake for a swim.

"Let's go to the other side," I shouted.

"OK" he responded.

So I headed out (it was about a mile across). After a while I looked back and he wasn't there, so I decided to go on my own. When I got to the other side, he was there with the car, shaking his head at this crazy kid.

Finally, another swimming story, this time at the lake in St. Croix Falls, Wisconsin. A bunch of us were on a picnic as part of the big prom weekend at school. When I dove into the lake, little did I know that there was a huge bolder just below the surface. Crack went my head and I was out for a moment, but recovered, although I had a very sore head for a while.

Was God watching over me through all of this? You bet He was and no doubt wondering what foolish thing would come next.

Golf Career

During the summer of my seventeenth year, I aspired to be a professional golfer. I had been to the St. Paul Open a number of times (sneaked in over the railroad tracks) when I watched Dr. Cary Middlecoff, Jimmy Demaret, and others play. I identified with a man who was a pro and had a business -- a driving range. I practiced a lot that summer and got my game into fairly good shape when I got hit in the head with a golf club -- a driver used by someone with a bad swing on the stand next to me. I ended up in an ambulance and was taken to Bethesda Hospital, lost two pints of blood, and had a very sore head with over 20 stitches over the temple on my left side. The doc held up a mirror to my head and asked, "Do you want to see your scull? You are a very lucky man, half an inch lower and you may have died."

It was late summer and football practice was about to start. I had this huge head, and they had to get a special helmet for me. But that was the end of my desire to join the pro tour, though I have followed it for years. Before ordination I thought the perfect job would be a chaplain on the PGA Tour.

3. THE SHAPING OF A LEADER

4-H CLUB, LUTHER LEAGUE AND COLLEGE

4-H Club

When I was 12 years old, a 4-H Club was started in our town, and I was among those who joined. 4-H Clubs had primarily been a rural movement, but in Ramsey County it was primarily a suburban phenomenon. There were many ribbons, pins and awards, but these were secondary to the experience of working with others.

In 4-H Club work, I learned teamwork toward a common goal, how to conduct a meeting, how to demonstrate, how to put records together, "To Make the Best Better." It became the training ground for many of the skills I would use as an adult. I frequently met with adult leaders, county agents and civic leaders. I took an active part in the development of the 4-H County Camp, played on a countywide softball team, and sang in a quartet that went to the State Fair. My parents were active leaders, Mom was for over 25 years.

Activities

While I was active in high school most of the school year, during the summer months I not only worked but also was involved in 4-H activities. I kept 4-H up during the year, attending various meetings, but most of the more interesting activities took place over the summer months.

When I first joined 4-H, much of my experience was with the Ramsey County 4-H Agent, Clara Oberg. Clara worked long hours during the summertime for many years. Because of her long-time leadership, she had carved a solid place for herself in 4-H Club work. She was Mrs. 4-H as far as Ramsey County members were concerned, and what she said was pretty much looked upon as law.

I generally had a good relationship with her and helped out at the 4-H office on occasion. She took a group of four of us up to the 4-H Camp in St. Louis County (a showpiece) for a couple of days in 1949. I remember most vividly meeting Jack Dempsey there and staying overnight with Mrs. Oberg and the other 4-Hers in a cabin somewhere out in the forest. She was also club agent when I went to conservation and health camps, demonstrated at the State Fair, and took a leadership role in the countywide organization.

Camp

On the north end of White Bear Lake just a block and a half from the lake was the location of the 4-H Club Camp where our summer activities focused for several years. The annual "booya" was a big occasion. A few of us came the day before to prepare the various types of food to be placed into the mixture. Potatoes, carrots, and rutabagas … in fact just about everything but the kitchen sink went into the mixture that cooked all night. We took shifts, and during the night the meat would be added, beef, pork and chicken, etc. By morning all was ready and people began to arrive to partake of the mixture. "Delicious" they would declare, "the best yet," or "next year you should add some turkey." It was the fall of the year, winter was not far away. The leaves were turning or had fallen. It was a happy time for sharing stories.

During the summer we had camp for the youngsters and for the youth. I participated in the activities almost every day, though I was not employed; yet I was conducting nature hikes and art classes, leading the singing of camp songs, helping out with dishes. During the day I worked at First Bank Credit in St. Paul, then I would hurry out to the camp.

Project

During my nine years in 4-H (back then you could be a 4-Her through your 21st year), I took up to eight projects per year. Home Beautification and Gardening were naturals as Dad was active in those areas. Admirers frequently visited our yard and garden. Conservation was something we tried to practice not only around home, but also through projects like the planting of trees and clean up. Health and safety projects were important too, not only advocating for the good practice of them, but also practicing it yourself.

I went to conservation and health camps at Itasca State Park. In safety, I was requested to sit on the Governor's State Safety Council composed of civic leaders. One year I was crowned "Health King" at the County Fair, along with Carol Mulstedt as "Queen."

As I grew in years I also took leadership responsibility. At first this was in our local club. Mom and Dad were leaders so it was quite natural for me to take a leadership role. Eventually, I was chosen for leadership in the county and state. We had a countywide 4-H leaders meeting once a month. I was asked to be president and gladly served. At the state level I served as president of the 4-H Club Federation on behalf of 48,000 youth around the state in 1955-56. This was a high profile job, and I was invited to speak on various occasions around the state. I had to limit my involvement in college, as I was frequently out traveling. (This 4-H position, plus serving as president of the Minnesota Luther League, made for a full schedule.) I enjoyed this to the fullest as I met leaders (both youth and adults) and was able to dialogue with them. Many of my closest relationships were formed through 4-H.

The position of 4-H club agent was dissolved in 1953, and was replaced with that of a home agent with part of that position devoted to 4-H. At about the same time, Roger Conklin moved on from his position as County Agriculture Agent. Charles H. Benrud was then hired as county agricultural agent and Florence Olson as county home agent. I worked closely with both of these people. They served well. However, I was able to identify with Florence Olson as she was the main person dealing with 4-H and seemed to have a positive attitude toward the whole program. It was a welcome change from the days of tight control under Clara Oberg. To put it succinctly, she was fun and I enjoyed my last two years in 4-H very much.

In my travels about Minnesota I met a family in North Branch that became dear friends. Harvey and Esther Schmidt lived on a farm outside of town. Esther was to become my "IFYE Mom." She recently passed away at age 96. They had two boys, Fred and Steve, who were in grade school. Esther was Chisago County 4-H Agent and had invited me to speak and judge at their county fair. She had a love for the program and good rapport with the county leaders. She was loved by the 4-Hers and was always out in front cheering them on. We developed a special relationship that has carried on to this day. She is now 95 years old and still active. I call her my "IFYE Mom." She had a unique connection to several that were involved with the International (later 4-H) Youth Exchange program.

Al Croone, one of her former 4-Hers, went as an IFYE delegate to Greece in 1956. The Schmidt home was a gathering place for IFYEs and like-minded people. The IFYE program was a forerunner of the Peace Corps, established after World War II to build bridges of understanding between peoples of different nations.

County Fair

The County Fair always preceded the State Fair. During most of the years that I was active, the County Fair was held in White Bear Lake. As far as exhibits or projects go, one had to place high in the county in order to go on to the state. 4-H leaders put a lot into planning the

County Fair, and it was a local show place -- much more than it is now. Top demonstrators and exhibitors went on to the State Fair.

County Fair was a more relaxed atmosphere. 4-H leaders kibitzed over coffee and shared stories; there was a genuine neighborliness. One day in 1951, I believe, I met Helen Hammersten. She had gone to her car and found it had a flat tire. I quickly changed it, and we chatted as I worked. Helen and I have been good friends ever since then.

Part of the Minnesota Delegation to 4-H Club Congress in 1954

Club Congress

In November of 1954 I attended the National 4-H Club Congress in Chicago. We were about 30 or so Minnesota 4-Hers plus state staff and leaders. We were joined by over 1,000 from other states. This was an annual celebration of 4-H put on by the big names of agro business. (Each meal or event had a different sponsor.). It was my first trip outside of my home territory, and the 4-Hers, leaders, and the personnel of the sponsors who seemed to have a personal interest in you, impressed me. We had a great spirit within the Minnesota group with broad representation from around the state.

We stayed at the Conrad Hilton Hotel, by far the largest hotel that I had ever seen. We visited places in Chicago like the Museum of Science and Industry and were entertained by personalities that we only saw on television, like Ed Sullivan! The food was exceptional as flaming desserts were brought in. The food industry wanted to share their products.

I was an escort in the National 4-H Dress Revue. National winners in various projects were announced. I had been selected to attend Congress for my Junior Leadership and was told that I was a third alternate for the special Eisenhower Award that was given to the person who won. It was an honor.

State Fair

The annual event of the Minnesota State Fair has always held a special significance for me, as it has in the lives of many Minnesotans. It is the last hurrah of summer, when the state celebrates its good qualities of living – horticulture, farming, youth, the out-of-doors, neighborliness, craftsmanship, art, and, as if all these could be wrapped into one, 4-H Club work.

Through 4-H, I was fortunate to be selected to serve on the staff of the 4-H Cafeteria. We would come early to get ready. Food would be delivered, dishes cleaned, and spirits soared high as we worked long hours during the fair when up to twelve hundred 4-Hers would descend upon the fair, all with projects of various kinds, from cows, to pigs, to vegetables, to handiwork to show. Some came to show their animal, others to present demonstrations, be in the style show, or a plethora of other activities – all of which made for the atmosphere of State Fair.

The 4-Hers all slept in one huge room. Five to six hundred boys (they did separate the girls) with beds stacked four high on the third floor of the 4-H building. The second floor held the cafeteria and auditorium, the first being reserved for exhibits and demonstrations.

Being residents at the Fair, we could roam about during our free time. We reported for work about 5:30 or 6:00 A.M., had a short break in midmorning and, depending on the work load, had a break of an hour or two in the afternoon. Later, we came back for several hours and usually finished our day about 8:00 P.M. We explored the various parts of the fair grounds: the horticulture building with the handy work of my father in the floral display, the dairy building where you could get free ice cream and watch them sculpt "Princess Kay of the Milky Way" in butter, the barns where one could see everything from prize-winning chickens to steers, horses, hogs, sheep and ducks. The hippodrome always had an interesting program, and the Department of Parks and Services had wild animals.

There were extensive exhibits of every type, including crafts and cars, gadgets and products for home, radio and television, and "Machinery Hill" which had the latest farm equipment. The sales staff demonstrated the agility of the equipment with a show in which they did a square dance. Then there was the "Midway," a traveling carnival with rides and sideshows of every type from the bizarre to the exotic. Afternoon races on the racetrack could be watched from the windows of the third floor of the 4-H building. Churches sponsored all sorts of eating places. There was an art show, and a romantic ride called "Down by the old Mill Stream." All of this, plus more, meant that we had plenty to do and see and talk about. The Fair ran for 10 days (later expanded to twelve).

I participated as a 4-Her in several events at the fair. Our club, on behalf of Ramsey County, had a booth one year that displayed the need for conservation. Dad was the main designer, and it received a blue ribbon. I gave a demonstration on flower arranging in 1952, the year I received top honors in the state for "Home Beautification."

There was an annual 4-H talent show at the fair, emceed by a popular radio personality, Cedric Adams. We had formed a male quartet in the county with Ron Chester, Dick and Ron Bucher, and myself. We had a limited repertoire as we traveled around singing for various groups. We won at the county level and then sang at the district contest, when we were supported by a busload of 4-Hers. The judge almost had to place us for the enthusiasm of our crowd. From there we went on to the state and Cedric Adams. Poor Cedric, we had a complication in our presentation when we had to turn the lights off because our number was "May the Good Lord Bless and Keep You" initially sung to a child going to bed. Problem was the child got stage fright at the last minute. We quickly grabbed the assistant Ramsey County 4-H Agent and I proceeded to kiss her "goodbye" in the dim light as we sang the song. In the process the whole system got turned down and Cedric was literally "in the dark" for a brief time. We did not get top prize, but had a good time anyway.

4-H Cafeteria

It was not long before I was the dishwasher at the cafeteria, one of the key positions. Coupled with the job of running the potato peeler, I washed the entire dish load for up to 1,500 4-Hers and peeled up to 600 pounds of potatoes a day. I had a crew of volunteer dish wipers, about 5-10 in number, plus the employed staff who would gouge out the eyes of the potatoes. Occasionally, there would be an extra volunteer on the crew, so we sent him or her on a "wild goose chase" to fetch a banana peeler for us. We had a great time, and the esprit de corps was high. As the years progressed I could not be there full time, but volunteered my available time. All told, I was there for 10 years.

The other event at the 4-H building was the annual 4-H Club Week, held in June just after school let out. Each county (there are 87 counties in Minnesota) sent a delegation for a weeklong event. The cafeteria crew for the Fair generally also served for club week.

Several State 4-H Agents who were my bosses at this time: Evelyn Harne, Elaine Christenson and Gwendolyn M. Bachellor among them. The State 4-H Leader during the years I was active was Leonard Harkness. He was an outstanding leader and instilled in us a sense of pride in being a 4-Her.

College

I was the only one from North Hi class of '53 to attend Hamline. I stayed at home to save money but this meant that my exposure to campus life was somewhat limited. On the flip side it meant that I would not face the temptation to crowd my life with all sorts of activities that would deter me from getting my degree. I recall the strangeness of going through freshman hazing. It was something totally new.

Starting out with basic courses, I was able to muster a C+ average. My academic aspirations were not high. It is interesting that the higher I went in school, the better my grades became. In high school I did just enough to get by and was not prepared for college, especially in English. For example, I had not learned how to write a term paper. When I enrolled in a five-credit geology course my second term, I received a preliminary midterm grade of D-. The teacher invited those who did not do well to see her. I remember her with great respect, a Miss Rand. I went in after class a number of times, wrote a term paper of "Weird Trees Around the World" and took the final exam. I came out with a B in the course! I will be forever grateful for this teacher who took me under her wing and spent the extra time with me.

Playing sports on intramural teams and attending weekly functions at the college kept my interest. Hamline University in those days had a first-class basketball team. Joe Hutton was the coach and annually took his team to the small college tourney in Kansas City.

I switched my major a number of times. I took more credits in art than any other subject, but I changed majors from teacher (art, sociology, physical education) to community recreation director, to philosophy. I ended up with a major in philosophy my junior year after deciding to go to seminary. I actually had more credits in art, but the expectation was that my training would be in philosophy as a prerequisite for seminary.

A fan, I attended basketball and football games, but my sport was golf and I played on the school team all four years. Senior year was my best, but I never really distinguished myself. I was in the band for a couple of years, in the Off Campus club and a number of other organizations, but a major portion of my time and energy was taken up by youth work (Luther League) and 4-H Club work.

I had a particular affinity to those active in the Art Club, such as Corrine "Corky" Swenson (who ended up a missionary to India). The one classmate that I admired greatly because of what she accomplished in terms of overseas service was Rozanne Ridgeway. She served as U.S. Ambassador to several countries before becoming Under Secretary of European Affairs during the time that The Wall came down in Berlin and "Perestroika" was operative.

The mid 1950s were years when America was positive about the future, but there were underlying problems that came to the fore in the 1960s. It was a time when a student could focus on studies, a passive time when life seemed to be OK. We were part of that group that idealized America and life in it.

College Profs

For some reason, my high school teachers seem to have impressed me more than my college professors. A few, however, impacted my life. LeRoy Turner, who did not fit the mold of college professor, but was an excellent teacher in art, was my main art teacher. He was a humble man who lived in Wisconsin in a self-built home that definitely was set up to accommodate his and his wife's art. They had a studio connected to the house, which was open, one room flowing into another. Robert Harrison was my other art teacher and the head of the department. He was rather staid, but knew his material well.

Mr. Thurman Coss was the college chaplain. Hamline was a Methodist School, so drew heavily from the ranks of Methodism. Bernard Graves was Chair of the Philosophy Department and my last advisor. He had on obvious joy in teaching, challenging me to consider what philosophers believed. Perhaps the most colorful lecturer was Richard Marsh, a history professor. I regret not taking classes from Scott Johnson, who later distinguished himself as a shrewd analyst of the political scene in America and overseas.

Though I only took one course from him, I was influenced by the life and demeanor of Clarence Nelson, who was a mainstay in the physical education department. He provided credibility to an area that was dominated by jocks and coaches and required measured goals and performance. I kept in contact with him from time to time, but never really adequately thanked him. He was understanding and flexible as my supervisor. Work (part time) consisted of paper work, but also got me to the various outdoor fields as I marked them and prepared them for games.

Making Christmas Wreaths

To bring in much needed cash for school, Dad and I set up a business of making Christmas decorations. We partnered with Hal Norgard, who had land up north with plenty of balsam and pine trees that he wanted to cut down. I would go north with him one day and cut branches (he also had a Christmas tree business).

Dad and I would set up shop in the basement as we got into the autumn season. We got the contract for the town Christmas decorations and had to have these completed by Thanksgiving so that they could be put up for the holiday celebration. Dad would trade his evening hours spent in the garden for this project. It was his way of supporting my education as all profits went to it.

We became quite adept at making wreaths. Dad had been doing this professionally at Holm & Olson for years, and I learned quickly. We spent many a night in the basement surrounded by the sweet smell of balsam. Even now, I can still smell it.

For years after that, Dad would make large wreaths, as he had for our home church, for congregations that I served. When he was no longer able to do it, I did it. For several years we had a church decorating party where I would show people how to make wreaths. Yule logs were another of our family traditions that we brought to the congregations we served.

Church Influence

The church definitely was a strong influence in my life. From Sunday School days on it seems like the church always had a place. Going to Sunday School and church on Sunday was a given. Grandpa Wendel was a regular at church attendance.

Mother taught Sunday School and Bible School for a two-week stint when I was young. At the end of the sessions, we got to take a book of our work home. I had one book, when I must have been about eight years old, entitled "God's Wonderful World." It included pages featuring missionary work in a large city, on an Indian reservation, in Canada and Alaska, in South America and the West Indies, in India, Africa, China and Japan. I don't recall that unit, but it must have made an impression on me that would lay dormant for several years.

I recall a preacher/missionary visiting and speaking to us about India. I was a teenager at the time but recall that he unlocked some of the mystery of India.

When I think of faithful service, I think of Pastor Rees. He always seemed to be available to people and greeted them with a genuine interest. What he lacked in preaching skill, he more than made up for with relational skills and hard work. Our little church on the corner of fourteenth and Margaret was soon bursting at the seams and plans were made for a new building right across the street from the school at twelfth and Helen. I was in high school at the time, played tuba at the dedication service, and sang in the choir (as I did for several years) led by Palmer Rauk. My years of confirmation studies (grades 7 – 9) were, for someone who was focusing on becoming a "jock' at school, not very memorable except for the tests with a lot of memory work. And in those days, there was always an oral exam on the day of confirmation that all of us dreaded. We had an exit interview exam in which I was mediocre, but passed. It wasn't stuff I was really interested in, like "What are the seasons of the church year?"

Luther League

Luther League was held on Sunday evenings at our local church, St. Mark's. We would have a variety of programs. There seemed to be a good feeling amongst the group, which of course changed over the years as some graduated from school and went out in the world. I held leadership positions and gradually became one of the counselors. In 4-H, I developed the skills necessary for leadership. In Luther League, I learned to apply those skills to a different setting, one where youth come together, more motivated by wanting to be together for service and personal growth rather than achievement. Not that 4-H was limited to achievement by any means, but by and large working toward a goal was prominent in most activities. There was nothing wrong with that, both had their place and I was happy to be a part of both.

There was an annual State Luther League Convention, usually held at Medicine Lake on a weekend in August. It was here that I gained exposure to fellow leaguers from various churches in our district of the United Lutheran Church in America. I was asked to serve on the team of leaders that planned various activities as well as the convention. I was assigned the Christian Vocations hat, which meant that I had to organize a team of workers and plan a major event, a Christian Vocations event. In this case it was in St. Paul at Rev. Charles Grant's Church. Grant was notorious as a pastor, for his quirky personality in part, but also because of his thunderous voice. Stories abound of his standing up at Synod Convention and orating on a particular subject. And when he prayed, it seemed like the whole world was listening. He ran a tight ship, but no one could question his motivation. He claims to have baptized more children than anyone. People rarely said, "I am a member of Faith Lutheran Church," but would rather say, "I am a member of Charlie Grant's Church." At any rate, at the Christian Vocations Day the idea was to place before the attending Leaguers Luther's concept of vocation, that all vocations are holy and to be considered valued.

I had it well organized, with an appearance by the seminary choir, and it went well. When the executive leaders who gathered in the spring of 1955 came up with a slate of candidates for officers in the Minnesota Luther League, I was asked if I would serve as President. Knowing that this would place me in the lead role of two statewide organizations at the same time, and knowing that I would have to limit my involvement at college, I decided to take the position. In August of 1955 I was elected and installed. I recall a telephone call home; "Oh no! Now you have two big responsibilities. How will you be able to manage?" I assured Mom that it was workable, though I wasn't sure how just then.

Trips

In conjunction with Luther League, I made two trips out of my home territory of Minnesota/Wisconsin, both in 1955. One was to the National Convention of the Luther League of America at the University campus in Ann Arbor, Michigan, and the other to the President's Conference at the Seminary in Springfield, Ohio.

Pastor C. B. Lund had invited me to ride with him to the national convention. I readily accepted. It was not only a free ride, but I would get to spend time with him, one of my favorite people. We drove to Lake Michigan, took the night ferry across the lake, and arrived on time to meet up with the Minnesota people. Judy Ford from North Carolina was President and a delight. One of the extra organized activities was a "round robin" softball competition. Minnesota entered a team. At practice I discovered the positions I normally played on softball teams (short stop, second base, catcher and pitcher) were all spoken for, so I said I'd play third base. It was a close game, but I do not remember whom we were playing. A foul ball was hit down the third base line. I ran to catch it, and the ball, my glove and my body collided with a chain fence! I was out like a light, sprawled out on the ground. When I came to, I could hear voices around me, "Is he all right?" "I think so." When I opened my eyes I saw Carol Jacobson, a student nurse and someone on the Synod Executive Luther League Committee. We started dating and became engaged. It was a delightful, but rocky road that we traveled. It seemed like an ideal match, but neither of us was ready for it and we broke it off the following year.

There were five of us from Minnesota registered for the President's Conference, designed to help statewide committees with information and ideas. We traveled all night, making the best time through Indiana state country where there was no speed limit. As president, I was expected to be present and enjoyed the give and take with other synod presidents.

Employment

The two summers following high school I was employed at First Bank Credit in St. Paul. The first year I was "mail boy" and the second year a cashier. I found out that I was not meant to spend my life inside adding figures and balancing columns.

It was during the summer of 1954 when a fellow employee of First Bank Credit invited me to experience flying for the first time. We drove to a small local airport outside of White Bear Lake, where my friend had booked a small two-seater aircraft. I was fascinated by the whole operation and care taken for our safety. We were soon airborne. He wanted to show me the capability of the plane so we did a number of maneuvers that were unusual, like flying in a loop. It was for me an exhilarating experience.

We talked about my getting into flying and the cost of lessons. He offered me part ownership in the plane for a modest sum. I recognized it as a very good deal for a small investment. It was appealing to me, but I was committed to first getting a college education. With that set as a priority I had to decline. But I was fascinated by the prospect of flying.

In 1955, during the summer, I worked at the midway YMCA in the Summer Fun Club program. There were about 80 boys, ages 9 - 10, who spent a good deal of the day with us four counselors. We usually had swimming and a time for exercise (workout at the gym). I was chaplain and we had a time of teaching. In addition, we visited places around the Twin Cities that might be of interest to the kids. A dairy, a soft drink bottling company, the State Capitol, an ice cream packaging plant and history museum were some of the places we visited. Then we had a week of camping where we spent the day working on related skills. All things considered, it was a good experience and I got to keep in shape.

When I was in college, during winter break from school, I also was a mail carrier for the North St. Paul Postal Department. At first they put me on a local route where I delivered door to door. I trudged through the snow merrily delivering the mail to people in my hometown. I had learned a good work ethic from my father and when I finished the route I went back to the post office.

"What are you doing here?" they said. "You're not supposed to be done until this afternoon. Go have some coffee."

After that they put me on a rural route where I went in a car with the regular carrier. That way, I had to spend the same time as they did on the job.

Church Camp

Pastor Rees and some of the "movers and shakers" of the Central Conference of the Northwest Synod of the United Lutheran Church in America had responsibility for the summer church camp at Green Lake in Chisago City. I was hired as "manager" of the camp, which meant, among other things, that I was responsible for registration, which started long before the camp actually opened. As staff, I had a lifeguard (Wayne Nelson), a cook (Mrs. Wold), an assistant cook, and a dishwasher who doubled as canteen operator. One year we had Sister Gladys, a deaconess, with us.

Prior to the opening of camp, we would have a workday when volunteers from the supporting churches would come and work on various needs of the camp. Then the week before the camp opened, the crew got together and cleaned the cabins and generally got ready for the opening of camp season. Except for one year when a big storm came through on the eve of the opening, causing quite a bit of damage (I recall raking the pathways with deposits of large hailstones that did considerable damage to the roofs), we opened without a hitch in June. Even the year we had the damage, we were able to open on schedule.

The rest of the positions were volunteers on a weekly basis. Pastors served as "deans" responsible for teaching. There were "counselors" for each cabin and a nurse assisted them. The manager saw that it all ran smoothly, registered campers, bought provisions, and was the general public figure to the community. I enjoyed this role and getting to know people like Roy Knoff, the local butcher, and the Petersons, whose farm I visited to get potatoes. In the summertime I preached at the local Scandinavian Church, Zion. I was with the camp "Board" (the official hiring agency) for two years, 1956 and 1958.

At the "Sons for the Ministry" retreat 1955

The Call

My call to ordained ministry was not dramatic. Over a period of a year or so, corresponding with the time when I was chosen to be President of the Minnesota Luther League and the Minnesota 4-H Federation,

I had been considering the possibility of attending seminary/preparing for ministry. At one of the "Sons for the Ministry" retreats when I was leading a Bible study on Matthew 25 (the parable of the talents), it became clear to me. I had been blessed with several talents, like the servant who had received five talents. I was to use them in service to the Master. God could take what I had and make of it one who would be given even more as a pastor. Humbly I prayed about it, and God showed me, through scripture, that He indeed had a place for me to serve. It was, I thoroughly believed, the work of the Holy Spirit.

Further research in the Word only confirmed what I had been led to believe. I spoke with Pastor Rees, who had earlier suggested that I consider it. From that point on I became involved like never before at church, as liturgist, as advisor to youth, as assistant Sunday School superintendent, as one who visited homes for stewardship. I was the third "son" for the ministry from St. Mark's Lutheran Church. The first, from another era, was John Shannon, the second was Dick Hamlin who married Pastor Rees' daughter, Janey, and was in my sister's class at school.

As word got out that I had made a decision, several people who knew me well indicated that they had been praying that this would happen. Dr. C. B. Lund, the synod staff person responsible for youth ministry and with whom I had spent a good deal of time, was particularly pleased and supportive.

The Master Potter was at work. The church had been a major influence in my life. It would soon become my bride in service.

4. THE SHAPING OF AN INTERNATIONAL CITIZEN

IFYE

The IFYE (International Four-H Youth Exchange) experience had a profound influence on my life. A forerunner of the Peace Corps, this grass roots level exchange program aimed at building bridges of understanding between peoples, opened up the world for me. Until that time, my view of life was confined to the Midwest. IFYE allowed me the privilege of seeing other people, nations and cultures in a new light. I was able to see a different view of the world and speak a different language. I saw my world and myself in a changing light and developed a growing appreciation for other cultures. In fact, I was fascinated by the exposure to other cultures. IFYE changed my life, challenged me to take an honest look at the world and to pursue answers to questions, which I had never before raised. How does one adapt to a different culture? Function in a different language? What's it like to become a member of a new family? To live and work with them? It was a liberating experience! I welcomed it. It expanded my view and understanding of the world. I began to view the world globally.

It happened that my summer work was at the camp in Chisago County, so I was able to continue my relationship with the Schmidt farm family nearby at a more intense pace.

49

The Chisago County 4-H Club agent, Esther had raised the question, "Are you interested in becoming an IFYE?"

Of course I was, but there was a noticeable gap in my resume, that of farm experience. Most IFYEs were from farms and went to farms overseas, so there would be careful scrutiny of my application and interview. I spent most of my spare time that summer on the farm getting experience and learning about farming matters. My mentor, Harvey Schmidt, wrote a recommendation, which was attached to my application.

When I went for my interview for IFYE, the question of my lack of farming background was indeed raised and questions were asked that tested my knowledge of farming. They must have been satisfied, because I was chosen as one of five delegates from Minnesota. I was placed in the Netherlands, where there is a lot of horticulture.

I studied Dutch from old recorded records used by the Army from World War II and became somewhat proficient by the time I left in June. Aart Huyskamp, a Dutch student from the Netherlands, helped with pronunciation. Esther, who knew the ropes, walked me through the various stages of the program. During the school year I often traveled up to the farm, and frequently Al Crone, Kathy Steiner, and other internationally minded young people would frequently be there. We often talked into the night. The farm became my home away from home.

The cost was $1800 to participate in the IFYE program. To raise funds Ramsey County printed up a brochure, and donations from the public were collected. On the back was a photo and quote of T.A. (Dad) Erickson, the father of 4-H in Minnesota who was the Chairman of the 4-H Club "People to People" Committee. I was especially happy about that because I had a long conversation with "Dad" in his home when he turned 80. He was a good role model and very supportive of IFYE.

Graduation from college took place in May, so I had a few days to get ready for the journey before departure. Orientation took place in Washington, D.C. for two weeks in June. It was a rather thorough regimen in providing us what we needed in going overseas and representing the States and 4-H. While in DC, I did some recording of news programs promoting IFYE with Hubert Humphrey, who helped design the Peace Corps and who later became vice president. We were also able to visit places of interest in D.C., as well as getting to know the group going to Europe that year in June. Altogether there were over 100 IFYEs per year at the height of the program. There were five who went from Minnesota in 1957: Margaret Malacca to India, Iver Aal to Honduras, Donavan Johnson to Guatemala, Genevieve Carter to Sweden and I to the Netherlands. Gen and I were among the nearly 50 that sailed for Europe on the "Arosa Sky," an old ship sailing under a Liberian flag that was used for college kids going to Europe and took a full eight days to get to France. I was asked to be chaplain for the group and provided daily reflections.

There were three of us who went to the Netherlands: Margaret Foster of Michigan, Joan Skupe of Kansas, and I. We traveled by train from Le Havre, France, to Paris, and then to Den Haag. Mr. van Westrenen, director of the program in the Netherlands did an excellent job of providing homes for us, punctuated with breaks after each of our three home stays to debrief. As he explained, there were three organizations in the Netherlands, one Traditional Reformed Christian, one Roman Catholic, and one Conservative Reformed. We stayed with one family of each,

First Host Family

My first home was located in the Halameer Polder near the present day Schiphol (Amsterdam) Airport, near the town of Nieuw Vennep. I recall taking the bus and transferring with my baggage in Leiden, arriving in front of the Ooms family farm in the afternoon. The farm was several meters below sea level. One could look out of the second story window and look up to the sailboats passing by on the nearby waterway. The family seemed rather reserved, but welcomed me warmly. Djoke, the 20-something-year-old daughter, spoke some English, but my "parents," Meineer and Mifrau Ooms, spoke only Dutch. Their youngest son, Gertje, was at school, but full of challenges to be played on the American when he was off from school. Wieber, their 18-year-old son, was learning farming from his father, and Anton, a 22-year-old, was serving in the military and away from home most of the time. I entered into the family activities enthusiastically, having long conversations with father over coffee at night. This was good for learning Dutch and gave me valuable information.

I was given details of how difficult it had been during the German occupation, of the large number of Jews that disappeared, and those that were hidden at great risk. Vivid pictures of mass graves and of hiding places, along with his first-hand account really made an impact on me, and I realized how difficult it was during that time.

They farmed 85 hectare of land devoted mainly to growing grains. I quickly learned how labor intense the farming was and the premium put on each square foot of land in this country that has the highest concentration of people in Europe. A couple of hired hands assisted with the heavy work of harvest, so the two of them, son Wieber, and I were the workers.

All farmers would like more help. Our neighboring farmer was stacking his peas the same as we.

Jokingly, he shouted across the ditch of water separating the fields, "I need help. Come over here, and I will pay you one guilder more than that farmer."

My host father demanded that was not enough, for he also had an American working.

The other farmer answered, "I will pay him, too, in American dollars."

I recall how my host father would struggle over the weather (a constant concern in the Netherlands) and the timing of harvest. When it came time to cut, Father would bring out the tractor (a luxury that had recently come into the mainstream), cut the grain, rake it so that we could bind bundles, and put it on drying racks.

I remember as a helper being given a pitchfork and the task of throwing the hay (loose, not in bales) up to the highest point in the barn (which was under the same roof as the house). At that time my hands were more accustomed to handling books than a pitchfork, but I entered into this assignment enthusiastically. After working on an hour or so, I developed open blisters on my hands, bringing comments from the two workers. I was determined not to be one who gave up a task.

One of the reasons why I was so popular with the press and the Dutch public generally was because I learned to speak conversational Dutch. This made it possible to communicate with more people and at a different level than those who could speak only English. I had learned the value of knowing another language – a lesson that needs to be learned by many more, Americans in particular if we are to be effective communicators in today's world. Though I have forgotten a great deal, it is a big advantage, even today. For when you speak another's language, even imperfectly, it shows respect for them and their culture.

Encounter with Mom

I loved the people and what they taught me in my three host families and still remain connected to two of them over 50 years later. It's true they are reserved. Yet they can be most understanding when the situation merits. I recall an incident soon after my arrival in Holland. It was one of those days when everything seemed to go wrong. That was perhaps because I wasn't feeling very well. And that was probably due to loneliness more than anything else, or at least to cultural adjustment. Rising as usual at 5:30 A.M., I had helped with milking and chores. After breakfast we went to the fields. We were not particularly busy, which probably gave me more time to think. I told my host father that I didn't feel well, and he sent me to the house.

I went directly to my room and lay on the bed. My host mother, unaware that I was there, came into the room to get something. Startled, she gathered her composure and asked what was wrong. I replied that I wasn't feeling well.

Pausing and sizing up the situation, she replied: "Yes, I understand. You must have a good rest."

That night she asked me to help her put her youngest son to bed and join their prayers. After that I was included in more family activities.

It was difficult in the Netherlands, but it was good. It was at times painful, but it was educational. God only knows how much I gained from that experience. I know that it changed my life. The world seemed to blossom before my very eyes! It was as if I had a passkey to the doors of life and was opening one after another.

Second Host Family

Time went by quickly, and I felt very much at home in the Netherlands. I had difficulty reading the language, but got along quite well in conversation. Soon it was August and I was headed to my second family, the Van de Boogards in Vierlingsbeek.

This family was in the south, in the province of North Brabant. The southern part of Holland is predominantly Roman Catholic. They have a lifestyle different from their more conservative and Reformed brethren to the north. They are "happy go lucky" people who enjoy dancing and celebrating the Saint's Days in the villages. Work is there, but it is not to interrupt the ebb and flow of life in the village.

My first night there I went to the local celebration and danced with my host sister, Nel. My host parents were interested in finding out about this young American, and that interest was shared by Harry (the farmer son who stayed at home to take over the farming), Michell, who was a student in the gymnasium (which was the equivalent of high school and junior college rolled together), Nel (the 23-year-old redhead who was a teacher of home economics in a local school), and Hans, the eldest son and a clothing salesman and physical therapist. Life was incredibly free, and I was working closely with the youngest son, Harry, who was the person who ran the day-to-day operations of the farm. Father was more or less semi-retired. In addition to the dozen or so Guernsey cows, a couple of dozen hogs, and a horse (that doubled as a jump horse for Harry) were on the farm. The family land was divided into several small parcels (some as far as five miles away). The family also had a part of the business of a ferry that crossed the Maas River near their house, which probably brought in more money than the farm.

The story of this family during the war years is a particularly interesting one. Just south of Arnhem, where a key battle took place, and being near the German border, their farm was in the direct line of fire with occasional visits from the Nazis looking for male laborers or soldiers. My father managed to elude them, but one time he did not have time to escape, so he hid in the eaves of the barn. When the Nazis came, they tried to tempt the children with some candy to tell where he went, but they did not. Within a few months they would be leaving their burning home and farm behind them and taking refuge from the fighting. They returned and built a new farm and have a stained glass window depicting the scene as they left. The window has the family, with fear and agony in their faces, fleeing from a burning farm, carrying their belongings. This has served as a reminder of how God had taken care of them during this time.

I enjoyed this family who celebrated life so much in spite of the past. The work of milking cows and caring for the land was seen as a necessary function. It was a liberating and educational experience for me to experience this lifestyle in Holland. I took an active part in farming, but also visited schools and the various festival celebrations. Time went quickly.

Third Host Family

The Talsma family with two daughters (Folkje and Hiltje) and three sons (Tjitte, Jan, and Ede) were my last host family. The people of Friesland in the northern part of Holland are very independent and have their own language. This was a dairy farm in dairy country, where cows took on special status. It was quite a sight to see the cows all lined up in their stalls with fresh straw, their tails tied up to a special wire, and their history and production posted above each cow. Needless to say, they got special attention.

My "father," Auke Talsma, was known for his quality dairy herds and prize bulls. He judged local cattle shows and was well known in the cattle market in nearby Leewarden. Their home, which was under the same roof as the barn, was convenient but was the most meager in terms of modern conveniences of the three homes in which I stayed. However, they more than made up for it with the youthful vigor displayed by the children, the youngest being 17. Moreover, they were a family that was open to exploring other experiences. Ede came back from France while I was there. Folkje left for another farm experience, and Tjitte had been an IFYE in the States. During my time there, they also had a French girl, Doeje.

We had great fun sharing and joking together, but the work was also hard. While there I piled mountains of manure, broke down cement walls, fed cows, helped with the harvest of wet grass for the silo, and generally did whatever needed doing. They were a strong Christian family, with Father reading from the Bible at every meal. There were no modern toilets, and rooms were opened up to let in the cold night air.

They did not own the land they farmed in Hallam and later the boys moved on to more modern farms but one nice thing about the land that they were on was that it had a "koije" with it. The koije was a pond with overgrown vegetation so that when you went inside you didn't see what was going on outside. This was to make the ducks that flew into it feel at home. The sides were set with camouflaged chicken wire, and there were a certain number of tame ducks with clipped wings. At the far ends of the koije were entrances into an enclosed wire cage, and special seed was thrown out to attract wild ducks. They would enter these and when someone appeared at the open end, they flew into the caged end and were "sitting ducks" to make it to the local Restaurants for dinner.

My time with the Talsmas was coming to an end. Part of my regular task of cleaning out the gutters involved loading up a wheelbarrow numerous times with fresh manure, then making sure the fully loaded wheelbarrow made its way outside and up a narrow plank to a spot where I would dump the load. It was wet and slippery when I had a particularly full load, and it started to slip off of the board. In my attempt to keep the wheelbarrow upright, I slipped off the walkway and fell into the manure. Not only that, but the load of manure fell on top of me. Everyone got a big laugh out of it, and my host father said, "Now, Duain, you are a true Friesa farmer."

I was closest to Tjitte and grateful for the opportunity to reflect with him. We have remained close to this day. I spent much time with him and enjoyed his wisdom and quiet country straight forwardness, his willingness to enter into conversation with everyone, and his outgoing nature. But Hiltje captured my attention as time went on. I enjoyed her company and personality. We have a special loving relationship, and we have remained close. It seems like when we are together, we pick up as though we have never been apart. I know I always have a home away from home at her and Feije's place in Friesland. Hiltje became a schoolteacher, Folkje a nurse, and the boys all dairy farmers.

It was most difficult to leave this family, and I have been back for visits – 13 times!

On my last day on the farm we sang around the organ in the "kamer" (family room), and I thanked God for the wonderful experience I had had with each of my families. It could not have been better!

As IFYEs

As IFYEs, we had three or four weeks of intense introduction to all sorts of cultural matters related to the Netherlands. We met with Burgermeister of various districts. We visited museums and city halls, the 600th Anniversary celebration of the City of Hoorn, toured cities and met with officials, visited cathedrals, saw hundreds windmills and attended "Tentonstellings" (or horse/cattle shows) that had some quality judging and performance.

Besides this, the three IFYEs got together, compared notes, and generally shared their experiences together.

I was reunited with my sister IFYEs for debriefing. I really felt that I had been privileged to be in the best situations. The girls did not have the same kind of experience I did, having stayed primarily with the wealthy. I thanked Mr. van Westrenen for his leadership and assistance. Then we had a few days free. Most of us took advantage of this time to travel to places we had dreamed of. I was off for Rome!

The train ride through the Rhine River Valley was a panorama of Europe. I traveled alone, until I met up with some other IFYEs in Rome. As we came to the Alps, the scenery became even more picturesque, and I took pictures of a village and church that we passed three times as we wound our way up the hills. We stopped in Lucerne, where, after walking around town and a night's rest, I went to the public ferry that services the various villages around Lake Lucerne. I got off a stop too soon, but after flagging a ride on a small truck around the side of the mountain, I made it in time to catch the train through the Alps, a most majestic ride.

I arrived in Lugano and after a day there, I traveled to Milano, where I saw the Cathedral and Leonardo's "Last Supper" painted in a mess hall that had been protected during the war by sandbagging.

Then I was on to Rome where the film "Three Coins in the Fountain" had been filmed. I enjoyed the sights of Rome, especially the art and St. Peter's, but I found, as I had in the Netherlands, that walking the back streets, getting off the beaten path of tourists, was refreshing and liberating. After a couple of days, we packed the IFYEs that had gone to Rome in an overnight train . . . to Paris! After a brief stay, we were headed to board the Queen Mary for our trip back to the States.

Homeward Bound

WOW! What an experience! Being an IFYE was sheer joy, traveling to Rome and the other places was the frosting on the cake. And now we were boarding the Queen Mary, flagship of the Canard Line, for our crossing of the Atlantic! My elation soon fell to dread. On the first morning out I felt woozy, but went to breakfast. There were ropes along the sides as I made my way to the dining room. The table was set for about 15, with the sides raised to prevent dishes sliding off. Two of us showed up. I thought if I ate something solid it would stay down. No sooner had the first swallow hit my stomach than the waiter, who was bringing us tea, leaned over and heaved all over the floor. That was all I needed. I was sick for several days and ended up feeling the most comfortable on the upper deck where there was a breeze and I could put my residue in a bag. I recall going down to my room in the front of the ship (bottom deck) and trying to sleep. It was difficult as the ship rolled so much that I got tossed out of bed.

Somehow I dragged myself to Vespers (I was in charge) at night. There was some good sharing that went on. We arrived in New York in record time. The next morning was the "Welcome Home" breakfast at the famous Waldorf Astoria Hotel. Fully one third of our group of about 50 was sick as we made our way to the buses that took us to Washington, D.C. for our final debriefing. Warren Schmidt and Kathleen Flom were helpful in interpreting our experience. Mel Thomson was helpful. I said goodbye to Marge and Joan. Gen Carter and I got on a plane to Minneapolis. There was bad weather when we left, and ours was one of the last planes to get out of the airport that night. Pittsburgh, Cleveland, Detroit, and Milwaukee . . ., this was worse than a milk train.

At about 4:30 a.m. we finally came into Minneapolis. I remember how beautiful it was with the snow falling. We got off the plane, and I couldn't believe my eyes! There were dozens of 4-Hers and leaders there to greet me. They had spent the night waiting. After my Mother served breakfast to all who came and after conversation, I finally went to bed for a long winter's nap.

In my journal I wrote: "It is nice to be home, but I miss my families in the Netherlands. Thanks be to God."

Molding Global Citizens

During the years following World War II there was an obvious need for grass roots ambassadors who would be instrumental in building bridges of understanding and promote peace.

Initially started in Europe, it soon spread to other parts of the world. It was well received and was especially effective during the period of the 1950s and 1960s. In time, of course, overseas travel for youth became commonplace and the program lost the idealism of those days. The world has changed radically since that time. The IFYE program gradually was phased way down and plays today a minor role in cross-cultural exchanges.

But at least for a while it played a big role in enabling people of the variety of nations and cultures to gain an understanding and appreciation of one another. I personally am deeply indebted to the IFYE program for expanding my horizons and giving me an appreciation for people who are different.

The things I gained from IFYE:
1. Knowledge and appreciation for my own country and culture.
2. The challenge and opportunity to know a different culture.
3. The opportunity to learn another language.
4. The experience of living with families and becoming one of the family.
5. Appreciation for other peoples and the desire to know them.
6. The joy of cross-cultural travel.
7. Contacts that began a lifetime of connecting with people overseas (an extended family).
8. The challenge to become a global citizen with an awareness of global concerns and issues.

P.S. – IFYE

4-H and IFYE have meant so much to me that I feel I can never thank these two movements enough. It has been a privilege to attend national and international conferences, each with a different theme and a different program. I participated in 1956 when the National IFYE Conference was in Minnesota. After that I focused on studies and getting funds together by working and did not attend any conferences again until the year 2000 when there was a special world international conference in Washington, D.C. Then fully retired, I felt I could devote some time to IFYE. But I discovered that things had changed radically. Now there were all sorts of overseas programs for youth. Although none of them seemed to have the same purpose and ideals as IFYE, the reality was that the IFYE Program was waning. The USDA had withdrawn a great deal of its support and the interest of young people seemed to be elsewhere. The Alumni Association was struggling to keep the program going.

I was asked to represent our region on the board, which I consented to do. Then I was off the Board for a year and on again, a total of six years. During that time we struggled with the goals and purpose of IFYE and the role of the association. There were those who felt that we should be more active in getting people involved and in giving. And there were some who believed that the association should only promote its own program, which meant that in time the organization would die out. The solutions were not easy. A Foundation was set up but has not garnered a lot of support. The concept and purpose of IFYE is still valid. But it has become watered down with the multiplication of programs with goals that appeared to be more self-serving. It seems as if the IFYE program as we knew it has drawn to a close.

Recent conferences I have attended have been in Illinois, Ontario, Minnesota and Oregon. I attended the International Conference in Sweden (Sigtuna) in 2003, combining it with a visit to IFYE families in Holland, a visit with missionary friends in Sweden, relatives in Germany, and a trip to England. It was a trip that was most enjoyable, connecting with friends and family along the way and traveling with my IFYE brother, Tjitte, and my wife, Donna.

5. THE SHAPING OF A MISSIONARY PASTOR I

SEMINARY AND SCHOOL OF WORLD MISSION

Within a few short days of returning from Europe, I moved to Minneapolis and began seminary life. Northwestern Lutheran Theological Seminary had about 100 students and ten professors, plus support staff. Located at the old Pillsbury Mansion on Twenty-second Street South (Passavant Hall), the seminary had a beautiful campus. The old Pillsbury House, classic Gothic style, housed classrooms, offices and a quaint chapel. In the basement there was space for housing a bookstore and packaging facility for "The Word in Season," a synod published daily devotional guide that was popular in the country. The house next to this one housed the library. The house behind facing Second Avenue housed the caretaker (a delightful German immigrant who had lovely twin girls and was grateful for the second chance), and some rooms for single students. A block away on Stephens Avenue was the building that housed the synod headquarters and down from that was Stumpf Hall, just across the street from the Art Institute. Stumpf Hall (named after a former professor) housed most of the single men. Downstairs was the mess hall where meals were served. This was the facility that I stayed in for three years. Within a few blocks the seminary owned two married students housing complexes.

I started out rooming with Douglas Buck from Wisconsin. The next year I was upstairs on the top floor with my own room, one of only three. Naturally, we stayed up late studying so it was nice that one could get up at 7:30 a.m., eat, and get to an 8 a.m. class.

I was already behind by a quarter (we were on the three-quarter system), which meant I would have to take extra credit each term to catch up. I was content, confident that I was pursuing what God intended, that I could reflect and build on my IFYE experience.

My studies were the standard fare for Lutheran seminary students. We focused on Luther's works, with a smattering of the well-known theologians of the day, like Emil Brunner, Karl Barth, Anders Nygren, and Gustaf Ahlen.

Focus on Mission

As my training progressed, I focused on mission and ecumenism. I remember begin impressed with a movie in a nearby church that focused on the life and sacrificial ministry of Albert Schweitzer He presented a good model for others to follow. I was moved by how this man was touched by the Gospel, the example of Jesus, and set aside a promising career in philosophy, theology and music in order to undergo medical training in preparation for going to Gabon, Equatorial Africa, where he founded Lamborene, a hospital that served those in greatest need. I was attracted by the fact that he gave up so much in order to serve. His "reverence for life" philosophy was appealing to a young theological student who had just returned from Europe. He came from Alsace, France, where German is spoken. Later I visited Gunsbach, the village where he lived. There is no doubt that his life had a bearing on my future decision.

As I took courses at seminary and further explored God's call, it seemed clear that I was being called into world missions. There were the passages of Christ telling his followers to "GO" out and share the good news. In Acts 1 we have the passage where Jesus says to his followers: "You will receive power when the Holy Spirit comes to you; and you will be my witnesses in

Jerusalem, and in all Judea and Samaria, and to the ends of the earth." I had a growing passion to serve in ministry overseas.

Professors

But I was even more influenced by a professor. James Raun, the dean my first two years, was a saint. He hobbled around on crutches and you could tell that he was in pain. He contracted a severe arthritic condition when he was in India as a missionary. He wanted to stay, but the doctors said, "Either you go home now or we will ship you in a box six months from now." So he left, but his heart was one of a missionary, and he taught our theology course as a person with conviction. Once a month he had a small group interested in world mission over to his home to talk about a mission "field" or to hear a speaker. I made an extra effort to be there. He retired in California where he and his wife lived with his daughter. I visited him there later.

Dr. ACM Aulen took over as dean. He was a philosopher who had taught at the University of Minnesota, always wore a clerical collar, and was full of punch lines. He was not afraid to speak out and did so at national conventions of the church. In spite of his demeanor, he could enjoy a good joke.

A professor I really enjoyed was Dr. Doris Flesner. He was a church historian who studied the Ecumenical Movement. I was the only student to take his course in ecumenism, and we met on a one-to-one exploring the issues of the movement. He taught other courses on the history of the church and had an interest in mission. It was largely through him that I became a mission historian. The ecumenical movement came alive as we studied together. Much later, when I was missionary in residence at Luther Seminary, we team-taught a course on ecumenism.

Our president was Clem Ziedler, a man who had a very successful parish ministry. He also taught the more practical side of ministry. As I progressed in seminary, he was a strong supporter. He was the one who represented the seminary at all sorts of public meetings, raised funds, etc. The entire student body was male. It was much later that women became pastors in our church.

Blessed

I was blessed to have quality professors who cared about the student as well as the content of the material they taught. There was a good spirit in the student body also. And, unlike today's seminarians, the church paid for our education. We had to come up with funds for other things, but the basic tuition was cared for, a big plus for us as we went out debt free. And we at Stumpf Hall were blessed with a woman who was a good cook.

To pay for the incidentals and get some pocket money, I worked part- time at the mailing operation of "The Word in Season." We would work when we could, bundling and shipping specific numbers to various churches.

My contextual education site, a local church assigned to all students to gain experience in pastoring, was Our Redeemer in St. Paul. On the east side with Pastor Les Stine as pastor, this parish that I was later to serve provided me with practical experience in ministry. It had been a mission congregation and was open to my untested efforts. The rest of the time I helped at St. Mark's, my home congregation in North St. Paul. During my time in seminary I wrote a rather thorough history of St. Mark's. Most weekends were occupied with church work, although Saturday could be relatively free.

Studies

Studies were demanding, but not overly difficult, and on the whole I did well. I believe that my IFYE experience had given me some insight and maturity, particularly in European ecclesiastical affairs. While I enjoyed and benefited from all of them, I found the course "Mission and the History of the Church" most interesting as it tied mission with the historical development of the church. Theology was also exciting as articulated by Dr. Raun because that was always a connection to mission. We preached in chapel as we were assigned.

As part of our training, we had gained experience calling on people in the hospital one afternoon per week. We were requested to write verbatim one of our visits. These were in turn, discussed and commented on by Dr. David Belgum, our pastoral care professor. Our calling was at Hennepin County Hospital in downtown Minneapolis. This was a place where all sorts of conditions were treated, so we got good exposure.

Friday night was our night to go out. Because of my contacts in the Twin City area, my little brown book became very popular! Devotions at the dinner table were usually light-hearted, and the atmosphere was more relaxed. Those who had girlfriends definitely planned on seeing them that night. One of the local pubs was popular and was also a haven for students from the art school. I was out speaking about IFYE or up at the farm a good bit of the time. On Fridays I would pack up my washing (my sister had a washer and dryer and volunteered to take care of it) and head to the farm. It seems like there was always something going on at Schmidt's. We would sit up late discussing world affairs. On Saturday I would make my way to North St. Paul, my home base as I participated in congregational activities on Sunday. This gave me time to be with my family on a regular basis.

Choir

C. B. Lund, with Jim Bennett as assistant, directed the seminary choir. I was a member of the choir all three years at sem. Between winter and spring breaks, we would pack up and take a bus trip, visiting churches of the Northwest Synod of the United Lutheran Church. The 18 to 20 who were part of the choir were, by and large, diligent and put in a lot of time to prepare a good program. I sang in the baritone section. One year I was asked to be the manager of the choir, which meant I would work with the director. Clarence Lund had already selected most of the churches. My responsibility was to be the point person for accommodations (we stayed in homes), food (the local churches were to come up with menus), itinerary and such things as taking care of programs and the offering. I had the additional responsibility the year I was manager to lead an interview of some of the choir members speaking about life at the sem. Given the nature of future pastors to speak, this generally was not a problem.

Hitchhiking

In May of 1958 I hitchhiked back from Seattle, Washington, where I had dropped a car that I took out for a leasing company. I had a few days between the time I was due at camp and final exams at sem, so I thought I'd take advantage of the chance to see more of the states. I remember the relief of finishing exams in the morning walking to the leasing agency, getting in the car (a '53 or '54 Chevy), and driving, free as a bird. When I stopped, I had traveled over 600 miles and was in Montana. After a brief time in Billings visiting the Myers family, I headed toward Moscow, Idaho, where my fellow IFYE, Doris Schultz (of native American decent) was completing her teaching degree. We had such a good time together that I was late checking the car in to Seattle, which meant I was short on cash. I had a couple of flat tires through the mountains and was delayed. In fact, I had exactly $1.35! I made a call to Barb and Chub Elert, old friends who had moved from Minnesota (Barb stayed with us for several years while Chub was in the Korean War). This cost me a quarter. I picked up a late bus to Tacoma for one dollar, got a packet of gum for 5 cents, and spent the night.

The next morning Chub took me to the agency in Seattle where I could get the $50 promised at delivery. The following day I was on my way hitchhiking back. Chub suggested that a truck stop would be a good place to find a ride, so he dropped me off at one. I sized up the rigs outside and walked into the restaurant where there were several men sitting who might be truck drivers. One of them was sitting alone at the counter. I went up and introduced myself to him, pointed to an empty car trailer and asked him if that was his. I asked him if I could buy him a piece of pie. He agreed and we spent some time together. The result was that I had a ride to Coeur D'Alene, Idaho, and could have gone even farther. I could catch some sleep in the night on the shelf in the back and I also tried to keep the driver awake. Since it was night we did not see much of the majestic Cascade Mountains.

I was dropped off after breakfast and continued on my way back to Moscow to see Doris when I picked up a ride about halfway. This put me on a secluded highway – not a good location for a hitchhiker. I was happy when a couple of guys came along and picked me up, until I realized that they had been drinking. They had a fifth of whisky they were passing between one another and offered me some, which I declined. Outside of Moscow. a state trooper saw the car swerving and pulled us over. The officer was going to arrest all of us, but I told him I was not with them and he let me go. I had learned my lesson. Never get in a car before you size up the situation.

After some time in Idaho and Montana, I was back in Minnesota and at camp ready to go.

Summer 1959

I had expressed interest in serving as a missionary in the Lutheran Church, but I also pursued other possibilities. I had applied to the American Friends Service Committee (a religious organization related to the Quakers that was heavily involved in service projects overseas) about a position in community development in Central America. I had written to them about the position while at seminary. When I was going to New York to speak with leaders about service in the Lutheran Church, it was also convenient for me to take a day and travel to Philadelphia to talk with leaders of the Friends. I took a train and spent some time with them. I left feeling affirmed, but with turmoil over what was the best route of service to take.

Pondering this, I immediately flew to San Francisco to begin my job as chaplain at Camp Royaneh -- the Boy Scout camp that served the greater San Francisco bay area. A few days later I received word from the American Friends Service Committee that I had been accepted. After further wrestling with it, I decided that it would be better to complete seminary, but there was a strong pull to get directly involved with people in a hands on operation.

Over the next two months I was introduced to the world of camping, Boy Scout style. With several hundred Boy Scouts, there was a lot of activity. I had responsibility for organizing weekend services: Buddhist, Jewish, Catholic, Latter Day Saints, Episcopalian, and Protestant (which I was responsible to lead). I worked with a number of scouts on religious awards. I also arranged for table prayers, participated in camp wide activities, and served as part-time canoe instructor. The camp was located near the Russian River north of San Francisco, so we took advantage of the water. The canoe base was hampered by a lack of water, but we had enough dammed up to manage basic needs.

I became friends with the aquatic director, Jack Mathis, who was in medical school. When camp season ended, he invited me to spend a couple of days with his family in Yosemite Park. I was impressed with the stunning panoramic views. After a brief stay, I was dropped off to hitchhike back to Minnesota.

In Reno I spent a long time at an intersection waiting for a ride. I had my Boy Scout outfit on. Finally, when the stoplight was red, a family pulled up. To make a long story short, I convinced them to give me a ride in the back seat with the two kids. The next day I even convinced them that they did not want to go through Salt Lake City without seeing the Mormon Tabernacle! When they stopped for the night at a local motel, they let me sleep in the car and in the morning clean up in the bathroom. I played games with the children in the back seat and got to know the family quite well -- even ended up paying for some of the gas, as they were short of cash. They dropped me off in Salina, Kansas, and went on home to Arkansas. I corresponded with them for years afterward.

I got back in time for classes to begin.

Final Year of Seminary

My last year seemed to pass quickly. As I drew closer to the end of the year, I received a call from the Board of Foreign Missions of the

United Lutheran Church in America. As I went through seminary, I had an increasing interest in world mission. Mission seemed to be at the heart of the Gospel. I wanted to give my life to a cause that mattered, that made a difference in people's lives. IFYE had made me aware of the world. Now I had a message to bring to the world. My contacts with the board office in New York had been positive.

I had a growing conviction that I could best serve by using the talents God had given me on the international scene. The first discussions centered on a call to work in Argentina, but as I got closer to ordination the focus was on Malaya. The call to serve overseas was accompanied by a deeper understanding of a call that would be cross-cultural. It was a distinct call to mission. Fuller School of Cross-Cultural Studies describes this as a "second call," the first being to serve in the church. The second call is more specific than the first. Both of these calls were tied up in the call that I had received from the Board of Foreign Missions of the United Lutheran Church in America to go to Malaya.

Sixteen men were ordained by the synod at its convention in Grand Forks, North Dakota, on May 19, 1960. My sponsor was Pastor T. S. Rees. Judd Lundquist, the newly elected president, had arranged for me to spend the summer months filling in at Redeemer Lutheran Church in Livingston, Montana. Livingston is the northern gateway to Yellowstone National Park, a town that grew up around the railroad industry. I entered into ministry enthusiastically. I trained a class of adults, some of them receiving baptism; I also called on people, attended functions, and preached. Years later, it was a joy to revisit Livingston and see the changes that brought several movie stars to the area.

School of World Mission

I loaded up a small trailer in St. Paul and was off to Maywood, Illinois, a suburb of Chicago where the school was located on the campus of The Lutheran Theological Seminary. There were about 30 of us, all scheduled to go to different parts of the world. Families with kids, singles, couples, were all housed in one building. Some were laypersons (nurses, industrial technology, agriculture), some had served previously (India and Japan), some were fresh out of seminary (like me), and others had considerable pastoral experience. Most had not met before, but we got along well, perhaps because we shared a common purpose.

Just across the street from the School was the home of Jim and Fran Scherer. Jim was the Dean, and both of them were involved with China missions, where they met and married. Jim taught all the theology courses, comparative religions, history and generally kept the ship sailing on an even keel. Donald Flatt was a Brit turned American after marrying a single missionary (Ruth) in Tanganyika. He went out as a British public servant, came to seminary in the States, and returned to serve in Tanzania. He was the anthropologist and taught area studies. A person teaching Bible rounded out the resident teaching staff. I felt particularly blessed to have R. Pierce Beaver, director of the center for the study of the Christian World Mission at the Divinity School, University of Chicago, frequently on campus and the teacher of several courses. He was seen by many to be the "dean" of American missiologists. Jim Scherer would later become known as the "dean" of American Lutheran missiologists.

We had practical classes and daily devotions downstairs in a meeting room in the apartment house. After getting acquainted, there was an election to determine leadership. I was surprised and humbled to be elected chair.

I wanted to be the best trained missionary possible in service to my Lord. I owed Him nothing less than the very best. I entered into this time of preparation enthusiastically.

My first weeks at the School of Missions on the Campus of the Lutheran Theological Seminary were full of conversations with people going to many parts of the globe in service. This made classes interesting and relevant. We benefited from being on campus by attending chapel, using the library, relating to professors, and playing softball against them. As part of our cross-cultural exposure, several of us were assigned to Lutheran congregations in the Chicago area. I was assigned to a mission storefront church, known as Christ the Mediator Lutheran Church on the South Side of Chicago, a ghetto area that was being changed to high-rise public housing.

Pastor Klein and I made calls in the neighborhood. The people were poor and had little self-esteem. In some flats the water or electricity had been turned off due to unpaid bills, causing great hardship during the winter months. Often, rather than climb the rickety stairs, they would dump their garbage over the railing. The old housing had deteriorated to an irreparable state and the city was tearing them down to be replaced by high-rise public housing. What do you say to people like this? You try to address their needs, but they seem to be in a never-ending downward spiral. The church seemed to offer solace. As we worshiped and served communion, they were assured of God's forgiveness and love.

I recall returning to the storefront church after calling one night. As we sat together discussing our calls, we heard a banging sound that appeared to be coming from the basement. When we opened the door to the basement, we found two men dismantling the furnace! They were taking it piece by piece to sell it as scrap metal. Pastor Klein assured them he would not press charges if they put it back together again, which they did.

Train Ride

During the Thanksgiving holidays I decided to go home to Minnesota. By far the best way to travel was by train. Clergy got a reduced rate back then. It was good to share stories and plans with parents and friends. I was excited about my studies and the thought of going to Malaya. But soon I was off again, back on the train to Chicago.

About one-third of the way, we stopped at Prairie du Chien in Wisconsin. The train was crowded and I was sitting alone reading a book assigned by a professor. A young brunette came aboard, lugging her suitcase, and asked if the seat next to me was taken. I said no and helped her get the suitcase on the rack. She promptly excused herself, and I sat back reading my book. She returned, introduced herself as Marcie Bush. She noticed the book I was reading and commented that she always wanted to be a missionary.

We spoke of her background and work and of the School of Missions. I learned that she was from Elkader, Iowa and had been home for the holidays. She had attended and dropped out of college. Time seemed to fly and before long I was at the stop where I was to be picked up (last stop before Chicago).

I had asked her if she would like to go out and she had indicated affirmatively. But in the first couple of calls, she seemed preoccupied. I decided to call one more time and this time she accepted an invitation where I took her to the school Christmas party at Jim and Fran Scherer's. You can imagine the questions people had.

I went home for Christmas and had a time of reflection, but as I was focused on overseas service, thoughts naturally went to with whom I would share that calling. The single guys at the School of Missions had discussed the pros and cons of being single versus that of marriage on the mission field. It was interesting that all three of us were married by the time we went overseas again.

For me it was a whirlwind. There was all the activity at the School of Missions – studies, extra classes, preparation for going, -- but also this new relationship with someone who could potentially share life overseas. Marcie and I entered into a period of intense exploration. She said that she wanted to be a missionary, but her lifestyle did not indicate that. In spite of the fact that there were some red flags, we became engaged. My desire to find someone to share my missionary service was acute.

We were married, in Elkader, in April. Marcie was a very dramatic person with a flair for the dramatics of life. She seemed to love the idea of the role of missionary wife. For my part, I was not ready for the role of husband, though I was for the role of missionary.

When the missionaries left school and went off to various overseas assignments, we stayed on in the States for a short-term assignment in Milwaukee, where I took a parish as interim pastor at Incarnation Lutheran Church, a church in transition. The idea was to give us some time to settle in our relationship before going overseas. It was only partly successful. Marcie became pregnant.

Board Practice

We went out as missionaries of the United Lutheran Church in America (soon to merge into the Lutheran Church in America) with headquarters in New York. Marcie had to undergo testing, like everyone else. Part of the testing was a psychological exam. Something came up on this exam that concerned those who were examining, the details of which were never really explained to us. As a result, we were asked to delay our going into the field over the summer. We looked at this as time to get better prepared for going.

We were commissioned at St. Mark's Lutheran Church in North St. Paul in August, 1961. David L. Vikner, the new Asia Secretary for the Board of Foreign Mission was preaching. His text was Paul's Macedonian call. He compared the action of the group that requested help in Malaya in outreach among the Chinese to the call that the Spirit gave Paul to come to Macedonia. Also speaking was Dr. Paul Graf of Holy Trinity Lutheran Church in Minneapolis, chairman of the board, and friend. Pastor Rees was Pastor Loci. When Marcie and I went forward for the laying on of hands, I felt a real presence of God calling us to serve in Malaya. We were soon on our way, visiting my IFYE families in the Netherlands en route.

A Valuable Experiment

The School of Missions was an experiment. Only in existence a few short years (less than twenty), it had a profound effect on the preparedness of missionaries. Anthropology, theology of mission, history of mission, comparative religion, linguistics, area studies, history of the younger churches, and ecumenism were all covered. There were informal workshops on equipment, packing, travel, and health. Spiritual life focused around evening devotions. The school was located on the campus of the Chicago Lutheran Theological Seminary in Maywood, Illinois.

Underlying our call was a common goal. Out of the experience of the power of Christ in our lives, as sinners in our own frailty but realizing our common redemption through Christ, each felt the compulsion to share this message of joy. There was an air of Christian gladness and anticipation as we went about our daily tasks of preparing for service.

I was appreciative of the time I spent at the school. It allowed me to prepare for overseas service in a caring atmosphere. As time went on, I found that I was well prepared for missionary service, but ill prepared for marriage.

On our trip to Malaya we were able to stop in Geneva at the head-quarters of the Lutheran World Federation and The World Council of Churches, where I was privileged to meet Dr. W. A. Visser't Hooft. It was a day off for staff and they had gathered for an informal picnic when we were introduced to this giant of the ecumenical movement that I had studied about in seminary. I was a bit tongue tied over this sudden introduction and must have left the impression of a young theological student smitten at meeting this man.

We also made a brief stop in Jordan before the six-day war and the occupation of Jerusalem by Israel. My contact there was Musa Allamay, a Palestinian who ran a vocational training school outside of Jericho. It was a great joy to see the work among Palestinian youth.

6. THE SHAPING OF A MISSIONARY PASTOR II

MALAYA

Finally we were in Malaya (which was merged into the larger Malaysia in 1963.) In western Malaysia (that part of the country that is the southern most extension of Asia), Malaysian society offered us a unique opportunity to get to know a variety of Asian peoples. It was exciting to be part of a society with such a diverse population and a challenge to get to know each of them.

Malays were the persons who had the long history in the country (other than the aborigines who where the original inhabitants). They were people of the land who owned most of the land that they farmed and were content with the relaxed life style they had. In time they became dominated by western powers culminating in British rule. Their language, Bahasa, or Malay, is now the national language. It is spoken in the bazaar and is relatively easy to learn.

Malays are Muslim by law and their religion is protected by laws. Officially, each state has a sultan who is religious head of state. The King is elected from among the sultans. The Malays are slightly over half of the population. Because they have been a non-aggressive society, laws were passed to protect their rights. Examples of this are that seats at the university are reserved for Malays and only they are allowed to own certain lands. They have controlled government and the military structure since independence.

Malays have a well-established cultural system that dictates behavior. They are subject to a special set of Islamic laws. For example, during the month of Ramadan, they are forbidden to take food during daylight hours. Their national dress, especially the sarong and kebaya, among women, is readily recognizable. Their relaxed life makes for a relaxed society.

The Chinese have been part of several generations who have migrated from southern China over the years. They settled into towns and became shop keepers and business leaders. They control the economy. They tend to be industrious and ambitious, place a strong value on education, and support their clan. For example, there are distinct practices that the Hakka Chinese will celebrate that other clans do not. There are several different Chinese groups, each represented by their own language. They brought customs with them from their homeland that determine their action at public and private functions. They work hard and celebrate major events like weddings with gusto. Chinese New Year is a time when they celebrate the most and fire crackers can be heard and seen throughout the land. Religiously, they practice a combination of Buddhism and Taoism. While men have taken on western dress, women have tended to wear more traditional dress, like the cheongsam that reaches to the neck and has slits up each leg.

The Indians are mainly Tamils who immigrated under British rule from south India, many of them as indentured laborers on the rubber estates. They are primarily Hindus. They have often been sandwiched between the Malays and the Chinese in making decision regarding the country. Indians value their culture and support persons from India who represent their ties. Today they serve in a variety of professions across Malaysian society.

Tribal people make up a significant part of the population, especially in Eastern Malaysia, but are represented by the Orang Asli in the central highlands of the Malay peninsula. These people have been isolated from most of society and have traditionally been food gathers and hunters in the jungles. In recent years there has been increased contact with other cultures and consequently a challenge to change their animistic world view.

In each of these groups, there is a number of Christians (although among the Malays there are few) who have accepted the new world view of life and who identify with a local church. Generally speaking, the various groups have been tolerant of Christians, though sometimes there have been hostilities directed against them. Christians generally have a loyalty to one another. They are about 12 per cent of the total population, although much less in western Malaysia.

How do all these people get along? There have been times when they have not and the country has suffered, such as in 1967. While it is true that each group tends to relate to their own people, there has been sufficient contact to encourage trust and acceptance. There is an intermingling of people at most public gatherings. National holidays tend to highlight acceptance of one another's ways, and emphasis is placed on getting along together at meetings, in schools, and in the work place.

This rich mixture of people provided unique exposure to life in Southeast Asia. Each people had their own culture and they influenced one another. Languages other than Malay, like the Chinese dialects or Tamil (the main Indian language), were spoken to persons who shared a particular heritage or culture. So we jumped in, eager to learn.

First Impressions

George and Frances Frock, who would become dear friends, met us. Those first months were important to our adjustment as we moved into temporary housing, got acquainted with missionaries, met students at the Lutheran Bible Training Institute (some of whom would become future Bishops), sorted out what our assignment would be, went on orientation trips to see the work, and took some Malay classes. The total Christian population (in western or peninsular Malaya) was around three percent. Nearly three-fourths of the country was still rich virgin jungle.

Moving into a duplex that had been vacated for several months gave us our first encounter with masses of cockroaches. When we turned on the water tap, roaches kept pouring out, and we ended up killing several dozens before moving on to other cleaning tasks.

Paul and Dorothy Alberti were located in the Kuala Lumpur area, as were Dave and Carol Eichner and Sister Gladys Reidenhour. Our arrival coincided with that of Bertil and Ingefed Envall, Swedish missionaries with India experience.

The Envalls came to provide Church of Sweden presence and aid in organizing the Tamil Indians. Up until this time the two scattered congregations of Tamil Indians functioned as Diaspora of the Tamil Evangelical Lutheran Church in India. Bertil Envall was warmly received wherever he went with lots of requests for assistance on various projects. The Tamil congregations had been instrumental in inviting the ULCAs beginning of work among the Chinese back in 1953. Mr. V. D. Pitchi Pillai, (a local Tamil Indian), Bishop Sandegren of India, and others had been involved in that important meeting in Penang.

With the coming of the Americans (plus several Hong Kong evangelists, some Europeans) work began among the rural Chinese. At that time the "emergency" was in full force, and the British were fighting the insurgent Chinese. The Briggs Plan was devised to herd the rural Chinese into havens (called New Villages -- 500 in number) where they could be protected and also searched before leaving for fields, thus effectively cutting off the supply lines of the insurgents. This created a new opportunity for work among the Chinese, and the ULCA responded to the call. But it was tough going those first years until a church was established and people moved into the cities.

Marcie and I (and I alone) made orientation trips to the Ipoh area, the Grik Valley, Penang, and the Selangor (around Kuala Lumpur) area. We were warmly received by missionaries and introduced to the leaders of these fledging congregations. We visited buildings recently put up and spoke of plans to come. Impressed as we were, we were perhaps more impressed by the Tamil leaders, as they were more outgoing and conversant. I had been called to work among the Indians, but now that Pastor Envall was present, some of the American missionaries thought perhaps I should be utilized in serving among the Chinese. Envall brought a maturity and persuasiveness that was hard to resist. I decided to work primarily among the Indians, to study Tamil and be the go-between for these two groups, which, it was thought, would be one Lutheran Church within a few short years.

Two brief diversions -- we had been assigned a car, a little two-seater Morris Minor with stick shift that had been passed from one missionary to another and was now on its last legs: We visited Grik, where there was the dedication of the Church building. During the same trip, we were privileged to visit an aboriginal settlement. The Orang Asli lived in little huts made of bamboo. They were very accommodating as we took photos and asked questions. I was particularly impressed that these small pigmy-like people did not yet possess the wheel. That would change in the ensuing years, but it was interesting to see them at that time.

The Tamil Indian congregation in Kuala Lumpur had a custom where they would visit members on Christmas Eve, caroling to each one regardless of how long it took. They came caroling about 3 A.M. We were surprised that our neighbors (mostly non-Christians) were so tolerant. Shortly after that we left for language school in India.

More Preparation

We had an excellent introduction to Malaya with its diverse peoples, cultures and religions. Muslims, Buddhists, Hindus and Christians, each with their separate traditions, were intermingled into a tapestry that was exciting. I looked forward to getting into ministry and settling into a home base. But first there was more preparation. We were to do Tamil language studies at the missionary language school in Bangalore, India.

We arrived in India before classes started the first week of January and moved into a small flat of two rooms in the missionary language hostel on the campus of United Theological College. This put us in the vortex of activity of the churches in India. Russell Chandran was principal of the college. The Study Center for Indian Society, with its director, Dr. Devanadran, was located in a nearby compound. The language school brought together a diverse group of missionaries from various traditions: Anglicans, Baptists, Catholics, Independents, and Lutherans, all committed to learning language necessary to work in their assigned fields of labor: the Church of South India, etc. Several languages were taught. Among them were Telegu, Malayalam, and Tamil. Mr. Dawson was our main Tamil teacher, and he drilled us for hours on end assisted by a Mr. Joseph, who, when he was sober, was good.

The Rt. Rev Rajah B. Manikam was the bishop of the Tamil Evangelical Lutheran Church in South India, the church that had diaspora congregations in Malaya that were about to become independent and form the very church that I would serve under. I was introduced to him when I did language studies in India. He was co-chair of the Joint Lutheran and Church of South India discussions that were underway. When I expressed interest in the meetings, he was kind enough to invite me to sit in on the discussions held in Bangalore in 1962.

Dr. E. Stanley Jones was an international evangelist with a focus on India. He had several meetings with Mahatma Gandhi and shared stories of faith with him. A Methodist preacher, Jones lived in Iowa when he was in the States. His wife no longer traveled with him and had quite a ministry of prayer and correspondence from their humble home in Clayton, Iowa. I visited her when on furlough and found her to be a humble and pleasant woman who believed strongly in what her husband was doing. I was privileged to hear Dr. Jones preach both in Malaya and India in 1961. His message, entitled "Jesus is Lord," has stuck with me all these years.

Franklin Clark Fry, a towering figure in the ecumenical movement as chair of the World Council of Churches Executive Committee, was also the President of my own United Lutheran Church in America.

He visited Malaysia in 1961 en route to the New Delhi meetings of WCC.

United Theological College

We enjoyed the college setting and interaction with students and professors. The college brought together several denominational groups, including those that were a part of the Church in South India, and remains to this day perhaps the most prestigious theological school in India. In addition to language study I took a course in Indian church history and a private reading course. On Saturdays we would go into the city commercial center, exploring the market place, trying out our limited Tamil, and doing some shopping. We met an interesting Hindu artist who was a student of Tagore. We visited his studio in town and shared philosophies and talked religion. I purchased a painting of his called "Husking" that for a time was in the office of the Board of World Missions in New York before finding a place in my daughter Hiltje Baskerville's home. Manishi Dey stood well over six feet, was single, and loved his beer. Once he visited us in our hostel and caused quite a stir. A delightful man, I really enjoyed him.

We, a theological student and his wife (the Macons from North Carolina), and a Roman Catholic nun were the only Americans at the hostel. In deference to us, they designated one meal per week as a "hamburger meal" when the cook prepared something resembling an American hamburger. As time went on, we tried to be away when that meal was served.

Kodaikanal

During "the season," the hot time in April and May, the school moved up to Kodaikanal, a hill station frequented by many Indian missionaries. The Lutheran missionaries had bungalows assigned to them, except we fell out of the loop for housing. With rooms at a premium, I was scurrying about to find a place for us about the time that Marcie was due. A British couple was kind enough to take us in for a few weeks.

When Marcie delivered she had the choice between the two rooms of the hospital: the pink room or the blue room. Not knowing the gender of the baby about to be born, she instinctively chose the pink room. The two-roomed Allen Hospital was especially geared to deliveries, and on April 18, 1962, Hiltje Christine Vierow made her entry into the world. The staff said that she was a real Indian baby with dark hair and olive skin. We were tickled pink. Francina, a young mother from Bangalore, took Hiltje out on walks every day while we attended classes. Pastor Bill Coleman baptized her at the Missouri Synod Church in Kodaikanal. Her godparents were Bill and Marge Fanning, who were in India at Dindigal for a term.

Van Allen Hospital was situated at the crest of a hill and Coakers Walk runs just below it along the mountainside. This is a popular walk for on a clear day one can see all the way down to the plains 7,000 feet below. At the other end of Coakers Walk is a church where Easter sunrise services are held. The congregation gathers near the hospital in the darkness and, lighting candles, proceeds to the church for the service. It was my privilege to preach there on Easter morning 1966 as the sun burst on the eastern horizon below with dramatic color and splendor. When the sun is moving to the west, and if the conditions are right, one can see their shadow on the clouds below. Our first home at Kodai, which was part of the single ladies quarters that we had to vacate, was right on Coakers Walk. We had some marvelous views during that time.

There is a long winding road up the mountain to Kodai. Located in the Nilgiri Hills of South India it offers some spectacular views of Mt. Paramal, a nearby mountain that is climbed by many. In the town center two roads met, one led to the town shops and the other around the lake. Kodaikanal School was located at those crossroads, spilling out on a hill overlooking the lake. It was around the lake where Hiltje was taken for many of her outings. The place where we eventually stayed was near these crossroads.

Taking the extension of the road from the plains, one would come to the Kodaikanal Golf Club. This was a picturesque place with a small clubhouse and 18 holes carved out of the hills. The first 10 holes were fairly well defined, but those following were rougher. In that setting in India, it was magnificent and caddies were always looking for someone to caddy for a round. I came to be friends with Manni, a young man from the community who was good at chasing the proverbial cows off the fairways and carrying my clubs. I entered the Championship Tourney and played well. The second to the last match was played against a missionary who did not seem to enjoy golf. It seemed for him to be an exercise to see if you could follow all the rules.

"Ah, ah," he declared. "You teed off beyond the tee markers, which is a two stroke penalty."

When the caddy master, who was referee, ruled that I was indeed within the markers, he was irate. Needless to say, I took great pleasure in beating him. My final match, won handily, was against an Indian man from Madras.

We were able to meet our Lutheran missionaries in India and later visited several of them en route back to Malaya. We got a ride back to Bangalore from fellow missionaries. During the hot season India is dusty and I remember breathing in the dust on the trip with the result being that I had a nagging cough for six months.

We worked hard and passed our exams before returning to Malaya. It should be said that Tamil is not an easy language to study. Indeed, it is one of the more difficult, not because of the 249 different sounds one must learn and the script, but because of the grammar. It is a very rich and ancient language, ranking among the top 20 spoken languages in the world.

Permit me to tell a couple of stories about life in the hostel. There was a British "warden" who kept things running. It was not the cleanest of places, particularly the kitchen. When we returned from Kodai, we started keeping Hiltje's baby bottle in the fridge in the kitchen. One night when Hiltje was fussing I made my way down to the kitchen and stepped into the dark room. Without turning the lights on, I heard and felt crunching under my feet. When I turned the lights on, the room was filled wall-to-wall with cockroaches. Sometime later I was ill and in bed sound asleep under netting when a cockroach crawled across the bed and into my mouth. I woke up spitting it out.

Attending the Desera Festival in Mysore

While in India we made a sojourn to Mysore for the Desera Festival, It was late in the year and we had heard so much about this event that we simply had to go. We were not disappointed and have some marvelous pictures to prove it.

The Maharaja of Mysore lived in a grand palace. This was one of those Maharajas who kept in touch with the people. He had been given the title of Governor of Mysore. There was a practice that on the eve of the celebration the people from far and wide would gather at the palace grounds to witness the turning on of the million lights around the compound that with the flick of a switch would usher in the celebration. We were there to witness this grand event, which was like a magical moment, especially to villagers who did not have electricity. In that moment a transformation took place. The entire palace and other buildings in the compound, the wall around the outside, and the temple were lit! It was truly a magnificent sight!

The very next day was the parade when the Maharaja, who was large in size, suitable to his reputation, would appear. Bedecked in jewels and appropriate robe, he climbed the stairs and sat in the elaborately designed gupta atop a huge and elaborately decorated elephant. The elephant was the largest in a whole line of elephants all bedecked for the occasion. There was also a band and retinue of the Maharaja parading through the streets of the city. It was a truly once in a lifetime experience, and I was to have a ringside seat! The morning of the parade we came to one of the gates at the palace. I had my camera out and ready when a member of the Maharaja's staff called out, "Yes. Please come in." I thought he was gesturing to someone else and looked around for a person to acknowledge the call. But to my surprise he was inviting me, Marcie and Hiltje inside! We quickly followed him through the palace to the very place where the Maharaja would appear to climb the stairs to the elephant. The man disappeared as quickly as he had appeared, and I was directly in front of the elephant that was awaiting the arrival of the maharaja. I snapped several pictures thinking that sooner or later I would be discovered as an impostor and ushered out, but that never happened. The Maharaja appeared and mounted the elephant as I snapped away. The trumpets sounded and the parade was off with me in it! I walked along with the parade until it left the palace grounds.

To this day I have not figured out how one lowly staff member picked us out of the crowd and made it possible to have this fantastic experience. I am just grateful that it happened. I would have gladly tipped that person if I ever saw him again, but I did not.

We worshipped each Sunday at the local TELC Church and learned of customs and church related events. I preached my first Tamil sermon there before I left. At least they recognized it was in Tamil. There had been one student of Tamil some years before who preached in Tamil. His wife, anxious for a reaction, asked the women what they thought of the sermon. The answer came: "Well, of course, if he had preached in Tamil, we would understand him."

Back to Malaya

After we completed exams in December, we made our way back to Malaya. First we stopped at the area of the old ULCA field, the Lutheran Church in Andhra, at Guntur and Rajamundry, where we stayed with newfound friends and viewed the mission work. Then we continued by train to Calcutta, where we caught a flight to Katmandu, Nepal. We took an old DC-3 that had the first few rows of seats occupied by baby chicks. Among the 15 or so passengers was Sir Edmund Hillary, who had been the first to climb Mt. Everest with his guide Tenzing. He had with him his wife and two daughters on their very first visit. We stayed with a couple who had taken a call to be pastor of the ecumenical church in Katmandu. The scenery was awesome and the people fascinating. There seemed to be more temples than people.

After a few days in Nepal, we flew to Bangkok where we stayed with Harry and Marion Kitts. Harry was a professor at the University of Minnesota who was teaching animal husbandry for a while in Bangkok. We toured several of the pagodas/temples in Bangkok before heading back to Malaya in time for Christmas. It was a good trip that introduced to us much of southern Asia, a relaxing trip filled with meaningful relationships.

Hiltje made the journey well; one of the favorite pictures is of Hiltje perched in a special basket on my back with Mt. Everest in the background. Hiltje was such a content and healthy baby and proved to be a good traveler.

On Christmas day I wrote: "As we looked back on 1962, it would in the future undoubtedly be described as 'the year we spent in India.'" The very word "India" almost possesses an overpowering meaning for us – its vastness, poverty, culture, customs, and religions have all made a deep and lasting impression upon us, one which we were sure would benefit our work with the Indians here. But most important, we had begun in some small way to understand the people: their problems, manners, and thought patterns so different from ours. It had not been an easy year, but then we didn't expect that it would be. God had richly blessed us with this opportunity and we were truly grateful for it.

We worshipped with the Tamil congregation at the church in Brickfields, Kuala Lumpur. Church leaders were happy to see us back, and we were eager to get to work. We spent Christmas with the Frocks at the Mission Guest House.

When we returned from India, we went to the doctor for exams. I was told that my specimen showed that I had 13 different types of bugs, including amoebic dysentery. With proper treatment and God's help, this was dealt with. After that, we took regular doses of debugging medicine that cleaned our systems out.

A New Challenge

Within a few days we were off to Kula Kangsar (about 170 miles north) a royal town where the Sultan of Perak was located in the Istana (palace). George had found us a house that was on the main road next to a gas station. It was a low house, so very hot in the Malayan sun, but George was able to get us an old used air conditioner for the bedroom. We moved in and became acquainted with the community. Just opposite us was a Malay (Muslim) family who became good friends. Next to them was a Hindu family and across the street was the local pig-slaughtering house. Just behind it was a Chinese temple. The slaughtering of pigs, while tolerated, was contra to Islamic beliefs but readily accepted among the Chinese. We got used to the squealing pigs being butchered at 4 a.m.

As we settled into our new quarters there was an air of excitement and expectancy. Kuala Kangsar was chosen as the geographical center of a new parish to be formed. While the Tamil church had few members there, it was central to a vast area where we would have several outreach programs, including Grik Valley, Matang, and Ipoh.

In Kuala Kangsar there was an Anglican church with a small congregation and an equally small Methodist group. We began worshipping with them and learned that there was no resident clergy. We decided to form an ecumenical congregation of Anglicans, Methodists, and Lutherans with a visit by the Anglican priest from Taiping once a month, the Methodist pastor from Ipoh once a month, and myself as resident clergy conducting the rest of the services. We developed a real sense of mission and respect for one another and took it to the logical step of having a common Sunday School and sharing expenses.

It went very well. The biggest problem we had was with the denominational headquarters. They kept asking us questions that we had already settled, and it became somewhat of a "hot potato." Locally, we managed fine, and I have fond memories of serving the people there. Mr. Roberts, the district police officer, was an Anglican mainstay. The Methodists, with their extensive school system, had several teachers.

This English speaking congregation of about 50, became quite a model but was not duplicated elsewhere.

This provided us with a local base for operation in the Upper Perak area. We had a "Sunday School" during the week at Leman Kati and Matang Estates and organized some youth in conducting a holiday Bible school.

I wrote the following story in Issue 13 of "Malaysian Memoirs," a tool for communicating with the folks back home that I kept up for 18 years. This will give you some of the flavor of rural Tamil estate life.

"Nneeh – Naaeehh! The young kid was bleating in my ear from the back seat as we started off down the road. Next to me in the car was an elderly Indian railroad lines laborer dressed in a new white dhoti. In the back seat crowded in with the goat were his four children and his wife, equally well dressed in a new sari. Today was our annual Thanksgiving Festival in the Matang-Taiping area.

"Nnaaeeh! How I wished that goat would stop bleating its problems right in my ear! I had difficulty hearing my friend speak. There had already been other services behind me in other towns. Besides, we were already late for our Thanksgiving festival, and I still had to pick up some other people. True, I said I would be happy to take the goat in the car and thus avoid their having to struggle with it on the bus. And, after all, it was being taken away from its mother for the first time. You could hardly blame it.

"As we bounced along the rough road past row upon row of rubber trees toward the estate labor lines (rows of attached houses), the goat had finally settled down. At last we pulled into Matang Estate and were greeted warmly by all – Hindus as well as Christians. Since we did not yet have a chapel we were to have our service in the small wooden Tamil school – the only public building other than the large open-air drama shed connected with the Hindu temple, where we hold our evangelistic meetings.

"Our service was scheduled for four in the afternoon. It was already that time. I knew it was futile to think we could get started by then. Time is just not one of the big concerns out on the estates. But proper preparation had not been made, which delayed us still further. However, our local members had decorated the school in many colored streamers, fitting for a most joyous occasion.

"At last we started singing Tamil lyrics, those lyrical verses of indigenous music typical of India. I never cease to be inspired by them. At our communion service we had the largest number of communicants ever in that area, 15 in all. All together there were over 40 present, excluding the countless number of children and adults peering through the windows and doors.

"The time came for the collection of the offerings: money, chickens, bananas, and a goat were brought forward for the blessing. Struggling with the goat in one hand and the offering plate in the other, I offered a brief prayer. As the faithful moved forward for communion to partake of the sacrament of forgiveness and reconciliation, I observed the sincerity on their dark faces, set off by the saris that draped the women. Now they came, barefooted (they took their shoes off as a sign of reverence), and I made an additional confession: "Lord, forgive me for my impatience." That was just one of the many lessons I would learn from these poor and humble estate laborers."

The members at Matang had a long held dream of building a chapel, but little in the way of funding. Their meager salaries could not support such a project. I encouraged them to gather funds for materials and build it themselves. One of our members, Mr. Ambrose, was a carpenter and volunteered his services. Other members helped and I was able to get the Estate to give us a small piece of land for one ringet (Malaysian dollar). Before long the chapel stood in the midst of rubber trees as a testimony to the people of God's presence with them. It was dedicated in December of 1964 and named "Bethlehem."

Kuala Kangsar

We were invited to community affairs like the secondary school sports day and the sultan's birthday at the Istana (palace). We shopped in the local markets using Bahasa Malayu, (Malay) the common bazaar language. This was usually a friendly encounter with people from the community, which I enjoyed immensely. Bargaining prices, especially when they wanted to raise the price for the "orang puteh" (white man) was a challenge that I cherished.

I would like to relate the story of a man who was unknown to me. He had an association with the railroad station in Kuala Kangsar and would see me when I got on and off the train en route to KL. Early one morning in 1964 this man came to the gate of my house. It was early and I was just getting up. He called to me and said in clear Tamil, "I came to tell you the sad news that your President, John F. Kennedy, has been shot. I am sorry." I thanked him for coming but could not believe the message. Indeed, it was confirmed and many around the world mourned. It was interesting that JFK pictures appeared, some of the Hindus placing the photos up in their homes next to Gandhi and Krishna and Gunabathi (the elephant god).

While in Kuala Kangsar I had a Tamil laborer for the railroad lines under my care. He lived with his four children in the railroad lines just a few feet from the train tracks. His 7-year-old son, Arul, took ill and was admitted to the hospital, his life hanging by a thread. I went to the hospital each day and prayed with them for his recovery.

Arul recovered and went on to become a member of the police force in Penang. He was feared by his peers as he was in charge of corruption and did not hesitate to exercise his authority. Many years later when I visited Malaysia, he recalled those days with great gratitude. Such are the benefits of pastoral ministry regardless of where it is. Arul remained single and in retirement started a number of mission related projects in Malaysia and South India.

We also organized outreach meetings in the kampongs/estates with films and guest speakers. My favorite, however, was when we had a

"Kalat Jebum," an event that had Bible story telling and the message of the gospel intertwined with music and comments by the speakers. This went on for hours. It was a special Indian form of communication which I am afraid is now a lost art. There was always a Christian group of singers singing appropriate lyrics with the story.

Being the main clergy for the ecumenical congregation, I became quite active in the Malayan Christian Council. I was on the planning team and a speaker at their youth conference.

About once a month I traveled to Kuala Lumpur for meetings. This was usually on the train. I caught the night coach about 11 p.m., got a bunk on the sleeper that was dropped off at Ipoh, and then hooked up to the K.L. day train in the middle of the night. When the train came into K.L., it slowed down for a bend just at the place where the missionary guesthouse was on Syers Road. I would jump off the train while it was still moving and have breakfast with the Frocks.

In addition to American Missionary Association meetings and committees of the Tamil Church, I served as secretary of a joint committee of the two groups (Chinese/American and Tamil/ Swedish). We discussed issues relating to a united church and mission effort in Malaya. These two groups, however, were diverse in history and ethnic character. Papers were discussed and general agreement over doctrine was achieved. But there was no agreement on ecclesiology, most especially the person and role of the bishop. The Swedes could not understand why the Americans and Chinese would not welcome bishops in historic succession as a gift, while they were more interested in who would be Bishop and for how long. The two overseas boards (Swedish and American) intervened and tried to make these divergent views compatible, but to no avail.

The Tamils moved quickly to organize into a church, the Evangelical Lutheran Church in Malaysia and Singapore, separated from India with a bishop in historic succession. They had their first assembly in January of 1963 but left the position of bishop open, pending conversations with the other group. The Chinese/American group moved ahead with their own plan to establish the Lutheran Church in Malaysia and Singapore in August, 1963. This ministry of just about 10 years was to be gathered into a church, an unprecedented move for the young mission.

A liaison committee was set up in 1964 with equal representation (I was chairman). A consultation was held in May, 1965 with Church of Sweden Mission and Board of World Mission of the newly formed Lutheran Church in America participating. The differences were not resolved, even though attempts at keeping a future merger alive were made. The ELCMS proceeded to elect Bertil Envall the first bishop of the ELCM in 1965. The two churches drifted apart in the ensuing years. This meant that my role had to be redefined in the new Malaysia (1963).

Outstation

My role as organizing pastor and evangelist included the Ipoh area as well as Matang, Taiping, Grik Valley, and Kuala Kangsar. There was a small cadre of members in the Ipoh area, a couple of families in nearby Tanjore Malam, and another two couples in Batu Gajah. We started a weekly Sunday afternoon service at a new Chinese church in the Ipoh area. Carl and Miriam Fisher and family were stationed there. Carl was a southern gentleman, who loved his Lord and a good glass of beer. Our families got on well. I baptized their daughter, Janiti, and Carl baptized my son, Dane.

So the routine was that we would attend worship in Kuala Kangsar on Sunday morning and pack up with the kids for our service in Ipoh Sunday afternoons. Occasionally, we would stay overnight with the Fishers, or with my golfing buddy, Harold Clark (wife Ann). A former butcher, he had a pipeline to some excellent meat. We got along fine and played about the same game of golf. Each year we would have a mini-tournament in the Cameron Highlands or elsewhere. Whoever was ahead when we finished was the holder of the "Clark-Vierow" cup.

Shopping was much better in Ipoh, so we would try to load up while down there. They also had a swimming club, a holdover from British days but now open to everyone, which we eventually joined. Carl and I had many conversations about the church and missionary life and strategy. He became like a brother to me.

Birth, Baptism, and Associates

Dane's birth in early September 1964 was a welcomed event. In Indian culture the birth of the first-born son is a big deal, so they brought gifts. When we had the baptism, the whole ecumenical congregation plus others were invited for a "makan" (meal) at our place. They spilled out of the house, over the lawn, and beyond. But spirits were high. Francis and George Frock were godparents.

Dane Christian cried a lot to begin with until we discovered he was not getting enough to eat. He was born in nearby Sungei Siput, a town that just years before had been labeled a "black" town by British forces because of the assignations and terrorist activities that took place there. Wei Mun clinic provided good care for him and Marcie. Dr. Mun and his wife, Grace, were dear friends and later moved to Australia.

Another task that was meaningful for me was that the first young Malaysian candidate for pastoral ministry, Moses Muthusamy, was placed with me for a year to gain experience before going on to the theological college. His grandfather had been a pastor who served the Tamil congregations earlier and eventually his father and uncle also entered ministry. This was a relationship of mutual respect that exists to this day.

One of our missionary friends was Daniel Nelsson and his wife, Solveig, Swedish missionaries in Penang. Daniel had been loaned to the Chinese church as I had been to the Tamil church. After visiting them in Penang, he said if I gave him the car keys, he would load up the 'boot' (trunk) for me. He really loaded it – with durians. Now durians are a much-loved Malaysian fruit that taste good but smell like an outhouse. During durian season hotels post signs indicating the durians are forbidden on premises, and the road home seemed to be particularly pungent that night. When we got home, I opened the trunk and found it filled with durians. This was just one of several jokes we would play on one another.

Danger

Perhaps the most dangerous part of my ministry was the long distances I had to travel, particularly at night. I would be traveling down a rural road by a kampong (rural village) and suddenly there would be a group of men sitting on the road, or a group of five bicycles leisurely going down the road, talking to their buddies and without any lights on. The general feeling was that if you hit someone who was Malay, you had better not stop. The word "amuck" is a Malay word. That's what happens when there is a fatal accident. The villages go amuck and take the law into their own hands on the spot. I thanked God that I survived those rural roads at night. Once Moses and I were driving home when we came across a man lying by the roadside in a pool of blood with his bicycle near by. He had apparently been a hit and run victim. We stopped and administered first aid to him. Then I went into town and told the police. They came out in a van and when they saw that he was an estate Indian, they lifted him into the back of the van ignoring all the medical practices associated with good first aid.

I was in one accident in Menglembu, a Chinese town where the Chinese Church had a resident missionary and clinic. It was in the evening, and as I made my way through town a bicycle suddenly jutted out between two parked cars. I hit the cyclist and she fell on the hood of the car, rolled off, and lay on the road. Within what seemed like a minute, someone had put her in a car and whisked her off to the hospital. Ray Nyce was the missionary in Menglembu at the time. He was a friend and knew Malay well, so he went along with me to the police station to make a report. The thing I did not know was whether the teen-aged girl was dead or alive. The following days I heard from the father of the girl that she had several broken bones in her leg but was doing fine. The father had asked me for financial help, which would have been interpreted as an admission of guilt by authorities. Ray visited the girl in the hospital.

Acceptance in the Community

How was I accepted among the people? I'm sure there were moments of doubts and questions by some people, but in general I think and felt well received. I was invited to local functions like school sports days and birthday parties. I felt free to go anywhere I wanted and talk with whomever I wanted. When I went to the post office, for example, I waited in line and took my turn like anyone else, although there were those who expected me to go to the front of the line (and would probably have done so themselves). I really felt that I was a viable member of the community. But I believe my attitude toward the people and open communication made all the difference.

I'm sure however, that there were times when other religious leaders looked upon me with suspicion and saw me as a threat to the established order. This was especially true when I went to the subdivision of an estate where several hundred people lived in isolation. One such confrontation took place between me and leaders of the Hindu community over the funeral of a member. He had become a Christian, yet remained in the community. We encouraged him to do so. I thought he deserved a Christian burial, but they wanted Hindu rites for him. I was allowed to perform Christian rites, though it might have been different if I was a local person.

Closing of First Term

There were several positives to our time in Kuala Kangsar: the congregation in Kuala Kangsar provided us with a local base for operation; from December 1964, we had a chapel on Matang with a congregation; Ipoh area folks gathered weekly at the new LCMS (Lutheran Church in Malaysia and Singapore) church at Happy Gardens.

Our first term of service came to a close the end of July 1965. Overall, it was a productive experience when I learned Tamil, got acquainted with the leaders of both Tamil and Chinese churches, and (though the attempts to get the two churches together failed) became familiar with the structures and areas of both churches. We were able to get two Lutheran congregations organized and into buildings and were instrumental in establishing the ecumenical congregation at Kuala

Kangsar. Our outreach programs were well received and we had youth from several different Christian traditions involved. I felt a real identity with the local people and communicated well with them.

When we left Kuala Kangsar the congregation had a farewell for us, at which time they presented us with funds to purchase a camphor chest that still graces our home in The Villages. The Lutheran congregations also had their farewells with flowery speeches and many tears. Our first term had been a good introduction to life in Malaysia. We had good participation in youth camps nationally.

We had all sorts of pets over the years, but in Kuala Kangsar we had the only monkey that was perched next to the verandah in a barrel. He had been mauled, probably by a tiger, and taken to the local vet. "The vet brought him to us for care."

First Furlough

Travel back to the States with two young children did not deter us from visiting missionary friends in Hong Kong, Taiwan, and Japan. We appreciated very much the kind hospitality extended to us and the joy of viewing work in other corners of the world, getting to know the histories and becoming acquainted with the settings in which mission was done. In Hong Kong we heard stories of early missionaries and the struggle with communism. In Taiwan we visited the student center in Tainan and in Japan we learned from a barber that Kagoshima was used as the training ground for the attack on Pearl Harbor.

Back in the States we stopped in California to visit friends, and then we visited Iowa and Minnesota where we had lots of people who were prayer partners our first term. I was particularly happy to see my father, who had Parkinson's and was in the first group in Minnesota to be placed on L-dopa, a special new drug, which I am certain gave Dad several additional years. When we left the States my father thought he would never see me again, so this was especially gratifying. No doubt he had thoughts of his departure from Germany, never to return.

We purchased an old car and were off to Maywood again to complete studies leading to my STM, Master of Sacred Theology, degree, which I received in 1966. But first there was a lot of studying and writing that would have to take place. I got a carrel in the library where I holed up much of the time along with Duane Olson (who became a good friend in Christ) and others also taking degrees. I wrote a dissertation on "The History of Lutheranism in Peninsular Malaysia and Singapore" that would become the definitive document referred to by future students. It was well-documented and accurate and 257 pages in length. In addition to writing I took some additional courses related to new missionaries at the School of Mission and spent precious time with family. Donald Flatt was my advisor because Jim Scherer was on sabbatical.

We lived in a duplex that was owned by the Board of Mission located in Maywood on a block next to the old railroad tracks. There were three white families in the whole block; and the remainder was all blacks with varied backgrounds. During a holiday period we were robbed but did not have much to take. We became acquainted with the neighbors and formed the first "block" club. This was common during that time and provided a monthly meeting of all residents on our block. We dealt with drugs and prostitutes, cleaned up yards, and generally kept up the area.

We got a real scare when Dane, still only two years old, reacted to the typhoid inoculation (inherited from me). We ended up driving through rush hour traffic, blowing the horn through red lights, to the doctor's office which was closed . By then the police were on our tail and provided escort to the hospital. Dane was in a coma by the time we arrived at the hospital. He came out of it, but for two days they put cold towels on him to cool his body. He outgrew this ailment in time, but we did have another incident in India. We were grateful that he had been spared.

We had no clothes washing facilities at our living quarters, so once a week I usually packed up our dirty clothes in a pillowcase and took them to a local laundromat. It was usually in the night and I brought a book along to read while waiting for the washing and drying to get done. One night I got all the washers going but could not find the book I had selected to read. It was a hand-signed edition of a new book by R. Pierce Beaver. I thought I must have left it at home, but when it came to getting the wash out of dryers, I discovered I had tossed the book in with the wash! It was quite a mess of small bites of wet paper attached to all sorts of items. R. Pierce Beaver, a friend and teacher, signed another copy for me.

We were able to have a number of deputations to local congregations, especially those that supported our ministry in Malaysia. These included numerous Sunday Schools, preaching, and evening programs. We were able to report of the ministry in Malaysia and thank them for their partnership. This also provided us an opportunity to observe the operation of a variety of congregation settings in the States.

Visits to families, while not as much as we would have liked, were nevertheless quality times of sharing and allowed grandparents time to spoil Hiltje and Dane.

In July, following the annual conference of missionaries in Kenosha, Wisconsin, we were on the road again, traveling back to Kodaikanal, South India, for nine months more of language study. We stopped in Europe to see my IFYE families en route. In our earlier studies we were able to complete the second year oral exams. Now we would focus on the much more difficult task of the written exams.

7. THE SHAPING OF A MISSIONARY PASTOR III

RETURN TO INDIA AND MALAYSIA

When we departed from Holland, knowing the difficulty of obtaining cheese in India, we decided to take a full chunk of cheese. This Gouda Kaas was round and weighed at least 20 pounds. We had placed it as the only item in a carry-on bag and zipped it up for the trip. En route we stopped in Athens, and by the time we got to the airport in Bombay, you could smell it several yards away. Fortunately, the customs official was preoccupied at 4 a.m. and waved us through. We got the cheese into India and on the plane to Maduri and on the road to Kodai. When we arrived there, we had the problem of finding a fridge because our quarters did not have one. The Granners, Lutheran missionaries who taught at the school, said they would be happy to put it in their fridge. Of course we indicated they could take some. Cheese was such a rare treat, the kids (unbeknownst to the parents) dug into it at the Granner home and a big chunk of it was gone the first day. Still it was good to have some of it during our stay there.

Hiltje and Dane on borrowed scooter in Kodaikanal 1966

Life in Kodaikanal

The Lutheran Compound was located in some hills a good half mile from the center of town. There were several cottages, some assigned missionaries of the American Lutheran Church and several to LCA folks. When we arrived, the season of the influx of missionaries was long gone. It would soon turn cold and damp. We were assigned a bungalow that had a huge bedroom, with bathroom, a sitting room with fireplace, and cooking/eating facilities. There were people waiting to be interviewed for the job of helpers, and we settled on Kanama and Kanapa. They were an experienced team. Each day they went to market and got our food and then prepared it for us. Kanama spent time with the kids while we were studying Tamil. It was a special treat when she got out her ceramic roller and crushed peanuts for peanut butter.

Things were a little sparse those months, but we had enough to keep us going. We only came with what we could carry in our suitcases. So Hiltje treasured her dolls and Dane got good use out of his matchbox cars. We were delighted that on Christmas Eve a parcel came from my parents with all sorts of new items for warmth, playing, and eating.

Mr. P. Jothimuttu, a well-known Indian teacher and scholar, taught us Tamil. He was one of very few who really understood the grammar, so we felt privileged to have him. When he had to leave, Mrs. Danapaul took over. Unfortunately, I took ill with hepatitis and was confined to bed for several weeks. We were able to get the last gamma globulin for the family so that they were spared. According to the doctor, I had one of the worst cases he had ever seen. Lying in bed for weeks I became quite weak, but I did get over it.

One night Dane took ill with a high fever, a holdover from his reaction to the typhoid inoculation in Maywood. For years after, until he finally outgrew it, whenever he got sick his fever would go up and up. One night after I had been in bed for several weeks, he got a fever. We took him to the bathroom and poured cold water over him. It was cold and raining. While Marcie stayed with the kids, I staggered out of bed and up to a nearby bungalow where we knew there were missionaries up for the week so that I could get a ride to fetch the doctor on the other side of town. We did not have a car during our time in India. As I neared the bungalow, I could tell that there was a party going on. Lyle Dowhower, whom I had never met, appeared at the door. When I told him of the problem, he grabbed his car keys and tossed them to me pointing me to the car and then closed the door. I went over to the car, which was a Landrover, which I had never driven in my life, and sat there trying to figure out how it worked.

Finally I got it going and inched down the hill, up the narrow road toward the main road. When I had arrived at the doctor's house (along Coakers Walk), it was close to 10 p.m. I drove up to the gate, parked the car, walked to the bungalow, and woke up the doctor. I told him of my plight while he slipped on his pants and we ventured out into the rain. He had a large "torch" (flashlight). I suggested I might come in the gate and turn around. He said, "No, that was not necessary." He would go behind me and watch the car so that I would not go off the driveway and into the deep ditch beyond. So I started to back up and he said, "Yes, OK. Good, come ahead." I could not see a thing but only followed what he was saying. Suddenly the car listed to the side. He rushed up to the opposite window and knocked on it saying, "Quick, I think you'd better get out!" The car was about to fall, and with the rains it could well topple over, so we tied ropes to the car and to a tree near by, securing it as best we could. We got a scooter and eventually made it back to Marcie and the kids. Dane's fever had gone down, of course. The next day, which was Sunday morning, as I lay in bed I penned a note to Lyle Dowhower explaining the situation and telling him that his car was hanging on the side of a hill on the other side of town. Years later I saw Lyle, who was then in Wisconsin, and we joked over the whole matter.

That situation set me back in my recovery, and we were facing the taking of our written exams. I recall staggering to the site of the exam, hardly able to keep my head up. By the grace of God, somehow I passed. Thanks be to God!

In spite of the difficulties we really did enjoy being in India again. The village people and their lifestyle, the Hindu Temples with their erotic sculpture and priests, the beggars, the beautiful countryside, the rich history and the way that the people converse with their hands, all of this was familiar to us now.

Kodai International School

One of the things I was requested to do was teach a class in art to senior high students. They were looking around for a teacher and someone had told them that I was an artist. We were limited to what we could get in terms of equipment. However, I was able to give the students a variety of experiences. I enjoyed getting to know the students and the school. The fact that I taught meant that I was now on the faculty of Kodai School and had certain privileges, one of which was access to popcorn.

Kodaikanal International School was a school that catered to missionary kids back in those days, although several were also there whose parents were in international business, U.S. Aid, etc. The campus consisted of dormitories for boys and girls, classrooms, a chapel, mess hall, playing fields, and a large hall with stage for events and performances. The school had chosen to produce "Oklahoma" that year. I was involved in helping out with the set.

One of the nights it was on, Hiltje and I had a special date to see the musical. We got all dressed up, and since we had a scooter for a few weeks, we got on the scooter and waved as we putted down the road and off to the performance. It was special for both of us.

On Christmas Day, 1966, the Troutmans, a Missouri Synod family, invited us to dinner. He was pastor of Lock End Church where Hiltje had been baptized. The Lock End compound was across the road from Kodai School. We had a marvelous time with the Troutmans, who were good friends and kind to us. That afternoon he took us back home. There was a crowd of people waiting for us. We had earlier decided to do something for the beggars and lame, etc., of the town that we saw regularly. We gave out "chits" (tickets) to these persons and invited them to Christmas dinner. Kanapa cooked that day for them, and we fed perhaps 70 or so in all. It brought new meaning to the story of Christmas for us that day. As each one thanked us for the meal of rice, a piece of chicken, some vegetables and a banana, we were humbled.

Another memory of that time is a trip I made with Paul Granner to Kerala. That part of the country was much like Malaysia in climate but was very different in culture. We came back through the southern tip of India.

I was invited to speak at the annual missionary retreat in Andhra. I recall feeling very inadequate speaking to these giants of missionary experience. Most of whom were my seniors in service as well as years.

Back to Malaysia

Our beloved Malaya was now part of a larger entity, Malaysia formed in 1963. Although Singapore had originally been a part of new nation, they soon left and the new Malaysia included both the eastern states of Sabah and Sarawak. These two states have a large number of tribal persons, so they changed the demographic picture of the country. Also Sabah has a large number of persons of Chinese descent. There are also more Christians in eastern Malaysia, over one-fourth of the population. So today Christians are over 10 per-cent of the total population. This means that we came back to the nation in transition, but one that would grow in number, but also economically (largely because of oil and the production of palm oil) in the years ahead.

Simpang Empat

The Diocesan Council of the ELCMS had assigned us to Simpang Empat (literally the place where two roads meet) in the Teluk Anson area. This was on the other side of the state of Perak, between the Bernam and Perak Rivers in the delta area. It was a naturally low-lying area so the water table was at best three or four feet below the surface of the ground during the monsoon season. There was a lot of asthma in the area.

The church was attached to our living quarters, which were attached to the quarters of the director of Bethany Home (at that time a home for about 35 epileptic children). Ole and Regina Solberg were Swedish missionaries who acted as director and chief nurse. Other staff included a teacher, cook and workers, in all about 12 in number. This ministry started when the church was started about four years prior to our arrival. Like Kuala Kangsar, the members were scattered out on the various estates. The central church served as a place for gathering and worship for those in the Simpang Empat area.

Our quarters were in the middle of a huge compound with space for expansion and sports. There were always people in the compound so our home became quite a grand central station much of the time.

We identified with the estate's poorer people, and much of my time was spent going out to them on the estates.

While I was working with these estate laborers, many of whom could not read, I was overwhelmed with their faith, often under difficult circumstances. People, especially those who worked in more affluent towns and with other people, would ask, "Why are you spending all your time among those people?" I simply answered, "Because they too are children of God and in need of God's grace."

Baptisms

In September 1968 after one baptism service, I wrote the following poem.

In number, 46
    those who came
        to be baptized
            on August 18 – a blessed day.

Sinners come to be washed
    stamped as God's own
        children to follow
            Him who gave
                for our sake.

46 in number
    potential for witness
        under God, unbounded
            by the Spirit.

They gathered for grace
    they are scattered for witness
        to the corners of this corner
            of earth – its salt –
                the leaven of the lump.

God be with them.
Count them faithful – to the end.

And we
    who continue
        to be used –
            sinful
    yet chosen
            unfit, yet of high calling –
                to praise and offer thanksgiving.

All glory be to Thee
Oh Merciful, Oh Master, Oh Lord.   Amen

A Half-Day

Perhaps the retelling of a half-day in my life is in order. It will give the reader a glimpse of life in Lower Perak during this time. Ulu Bernam/Sungei Samak Estates was a four hour journey by boat. I would take the local boat up the river (it stopped at various jetties on the way) and arrived late in the afternoon. Then I would proceed to the labor lines where I would visit with people and hold a service. There were always the sick to visit and various problems to deal with. I also had an ecumenical service for staff in the chapel at Ulu Bernam. Then, the next day I would return via the ferryboat, down the river to the place where I had parked the car. This was "Malaysian Memoirs" number 25, written in April 1969.

"It was still dark. I was awakened by the harangue of laborers going to their 'muster' or roll call to receive their daily working assignments. Knowing time was short, I jumped up and slipped into my clothes. After a cup of tea and morning prayers with the family with whom I had spent the night, I started to walk to the jetty (pier). Darkness was just clearing from the sky and a haze still clung to the oil palms along the roadside.

I arrived at the jetty just as the launch was pulling up. It was off again within seconds, and we were on our journey 25 miles down the Bernam River. The time was 6:50 a.m.

It was a good visit this time, I thought, as I wrapped a blanket about me to protect myself from the morning dampness. Our two services (one in Tamil, one in English) and "Sunday" school were well attended, we had a good class of confirmands, and we made contact with persons interested in baptism through relatives who were church members.

My thoughts were interrupted as we pulled up alongside a Malay kampong (settlement). The jetty creaked and seemed to lean a bit more in spite of being recently braced by several rubber tree logs. The kampong people chattered and laughed, greeting friends on the boat, and commenting on what was loaded on the boat to be taken for sale at the open market in a town downstream.

Two sampans crisscrossed in front of us, taking advantage of the outgoing tide to wing them on their way. The oarsmen, standing and rowing with long sweeping forward motions, jockeyed their craft into position so that the waves sent by the launch would be to their advantage.

The mist was still lifting from the underbrush jutting out alongside of the river. Looking ahead I was awed once again by the calmness and serenity of the river early in the morning. I was impressed by the rich green vegetation lining both sides of the river and reflected in the brownish-gray silt-filled water. Here and there the various hues of green were sprinkled with flowers and ripening fruit. The roof of the jungle and the even rows of estate coconut trees., could be seen. The high tide line was clearly visible on the vegetation.

The receding tide bared the roots of the trees protruding from the mud. One is immediately aware why this area is classified as mangrove swamp. Various species of brush and trees, mainly mangroves, provide an interesting study of roots. Some spread their tangled mass of buttress-like roots over the area, others send roots out horizontally, while others dig into the mud and then shoot ends back out of the mud into the air. Still others have roots that hang down from branches like long noodles.

If one looks carefully near the shore, an occasional crab can be seen as well as numerous specimens of a hilarious little amphibious fish known as mudskippers, but technically as "periophthalmus." These little fellows (up to six inches in length) can breathe perfectly well under water but love to play in the mud. They can easily be seen hopping, jumping, and skipping about and are even capable of climbing roots. But I know from experience that they are nearly impossible to catch! They look all the funnier because of their odd appearance. They are a streamlined torpedo shape and have bulbous eyes protruding about their blunt heads. When they are resting, their pectoral fins give the impression of forearms.

A few monkeys were mischievously playing along the bank, an obvious nuisance to the owner of the banana trees visible just behind them. A handful of swallows played about the front of the boat, landing now and then for a rest on one of the boat's beams and chirping. Crocodiles, common along this part of the river not long ago, are now a rare sight, for having given in to "progress," they have moved up the river.

I had long ago discarded the blanket. As the sun rose in the sky, the tropical heat brought more kampong people to the riverside for bathing and washing of clothes. Getting up to take a look around the boat, I noticed that among those on board was a woman in labor going to the hospital; several estate laborers and their families going on "holidays," probably to another relative; kampong people going to do weekly (or monthly) shopping; and children going to school.

I recognized one Tamil woman, middle-aged and slight of stature. Her graying hair was unkempt except to be gathered and tied back. Her poverty was evidenced by the fact that she had two small inexpensive rings in her nose, but none in her ears. The redness of her lips and teeth indicated she was chewing betel nut. A piece of worn cloth was wrapped about the waist-top of her sarong and slung over her left shoulder. Color combinations seemed irrelevant.

She greeted me warmly and struck up a conversation immediately. After the preliminaries of inquiry into the well-being of our families, she raised some important questions. We have had contact with this woman and her family for nearly a year. One of her sons was preparing for baptism. She had obviously been considering conversion. "Must I throw away my idols in the house?" "I have promised Murukan (one of the gods of the Hindu pantheon) to carry the kavadi (a burden or vehicle as a form of penance) at Chithirai Paruvan (biggest of the local Hindu festivals) every year for the rest of my present life (the Hindu believes in reincarnation)." I spoke to her of sin and the need for salvation in Jesus Christ, which she had obviously begun to understand. The meaning of God's love manifested and sacrificed for us, accepting salvation in faith, forgiveness and eternal life were explained in detail.

One of the most difficult things to understand for those Hindus interested in conversion is the sufficiency of Jesus Christ. Many will believe in Him and are happy to worship Him along with their Hindu gods, even place Him in a position of honor. To be safe they feel the more inclusive they become, the better are their chances for the next life. That there is One who is all that is necessary, who has already conquered sin and death, is a difficult concept -- so is the idea that we cannot gain our own salvation.

Seeing that the Holy Spirit was at work and she needed time, I requested her to consider these matters carefully and I would visit her and her family on my next trip. In the meantime I would pray for her. She smiled and thanked me as I left. I thought of how only recently this woman had been one of the most active mediums in the Hindu community in her estate, and what a glorious witness to God it would be if she would accept Jesus as Lord and Savior.

When I went back to my seat, the young Malay man next to me started a conversation addressing me as "Pastor," my common name in the area. We got into the subject of the meaning of Hari Raya Haji (a

Muslim holy day celebrating the Haj at Mecca, and a holiday when he would be visiting his family.) From that we passed on to the similarities of our religion, and the Bahai group that he knows about from his schooling days in a technological college in the capital city.

The launch was nearing the jetty where we would get off so we said our goodbyes and collected our barang-barang (luggage.) As I stepped off the boat, sweat rolled off my brow, down my neck and the small of my back.

As one comes down the road, the church compound is clearly visible with its complex of buildings including chapel and all purpose hall, parsonage, Bethany home for epileptic children, director's home and labor lines. As I pulled in, the kindergarten was having recess, an indication that the morning was already drawing to its close. The children – Chinese, Malays, and Indians -- greeted me with their usual cheerful "Good morning, pastor" in slightly broken English as most of the children are just beginning to learn English. English medium kindergartens, especially in the rural areas, are good stepping-stones and a "head start" to the better schools in Teluk Anson town. Ours was the only such school in the area.

Marcie already had breakfast on the table when I was able to break away from the usual groups waiting for me on the doorstep. The van driver needs petrol (gas) and wants to know if another school child can ride the van; our evangelist trainee is waiting for our class; a young man from a neighboring estate wants advice and support in forming a co-operative and for processing and marketing rubber, thus helping the small holder and avoiding the middle man; a member wishes to apply for a scholarship for his children's education and needs advice in the matter of finding a marriage mate for his daughter; a kindergarten teacher wants to give me money she has collected for school fee, and so it goes. Somehow I must get time for class, service and sermon preparations.

Back at The Centre

There was a flurry of activity at Simpang Empat with junior work, kindergarten, youth meetings, sports, church, Sunday School, and all sorts of special meetings. We would try to emphasize festival days like Christmas, Easter, Pentecost, and Harvest Festival with several planned events. It was not uncommon for people to come the night before and stay over for the Sunday activities. So we had special worship with confirmations and baptisms (ranging from infants to a 70-year-old grandmother). That would usually be followed by a drama and a meal prepared on site. It was relatively easy to serve food since they ate with their fingers and banana leaves could be used as plates. Then the afternoon would be filled with junior activities and perhaps a sports game or day of races. It would be a celebrative event when these Tamil laborers would be able to get together, share with one another, and go home feeling good about themselves and (for many of them) their newfound faith.

There were several youth who were important to the ministry there. For a while there was a Peace Corps volunteer, Janice Toby, who served as organist for our congregation. There were several Hindu boys who gave leadership, but mainly there were some key Christian young people who were eager to share their faith and participate. During this time two of the young men who ended up as pastors were baptized: Paul Krishnan and Devadason. Michael, another young man of promise, was assigned as an evangelist and worked closely with me. A typical day had Michael and me meeting in the morning and then after lunch and a rest, going out to the estates. Often this included contact with non-Christians, people who were seekers looking for meaning. Michael and I would lead them to scripture and gradually nurture them in the faith. Michael met an untimely death in an auto accident just prior to his retirement as pastor.

Outreach

During my ministry of just over three years, there were over 250 persons baptized. The joy and freedom this brought was astounding. We worked along family lines, contacting relatives of those who were

Christians and following up on those who came to us. It was such a joy to work with them, but also very demanding.

Regular weekly visits were made to the nearby estates. The 17th mile (where I contracted dengue fever – not once, but thrice) was one where we had several members and an active junior work program. Junior work was combination of scouting with a religious component that was very popular with our young people. There were both boys and girls groups.

Then there were weekly visits to an estate closer to Teluk Anson but separated by a river. I would take the ferry across and then bike or walk to the second division where we had several members. I recall taking the ferry across the river late in the day. I often sat on the top of the roof over the boat and took in the whole panorama. With the setting sun, the end of the day and memories of a day with these poor estate laborers, I would pause and give thanks to God for the privilege of working among them.

Other places included 19th Mile and 17th Mile on the Bagan Datoh Road, Simpang Empat, and the town of Teluk Anson. I very much appreciated the opportunity to work with S. Wellington, a great saint of the church and tireless worker who was secretary of the Council for many years.

Chosen

Reflecting on the theme that evangelism is "one beggar telling another beggar where to get food," I wrote the following devotional. John 15:16a: "You did not choose me, I chose you, and appointed you to go and bear much fruit …."

To be chosen
   by men
   is one thing,
   by God
   is quite another,

Chosen – set apart
   redeemed
   in baptism,

Appointed – commissioned
   you, oh Christian,
   to bear fruit
   that endures.

Impossible by men,
   but with God, through men
   a promise fulfilled.

So Love, man, Love
   is the command.
   Share what God has done,
   oh, chosen one!   Amen.

As time went on, we developed work in town and I was given the authority to negotiate for land on an estate that was closing. The Estate Manager, Alan Awcock, and others gave me a very reasonable price (M$55,000) for a beautiful site of several acres with buildings of the old estate hospital just opposite of the site for the new town hospital. The old isolation ward became the new chapel and we started a kindergarten in another building.

After a time Moses Muthusamy, the student who was with me in Kuala Kangsar, was assigned to this work and we moved into Teluk Anson.

Planters

Estate life was unique in the rural areas of Malaysia. Perhaps the most interesting stories where those shared among the "planters," who were a breed of expats (most of them Brits, but from other countries as well). These were men who were persons attracted to a high-risk life style. Most of them served in isolated situations, being top operations personnel (often managers or engineers) of European-owned companies. They generally lived in large bungalows, belonged to expat clubs and lived a life style that was on the edge. One engineer (Beck by name) was also a pilot and flew his single engine plane regularly between estates. Occasionally he would have problems over the jungle and crash, but was known for landing softly on the tree tops and escaping serious injury.

Another who became friends and someone I married, was known for grand prix racing. He displayed the steering wheel in the living room, the only thing salvageable from the wreck he had at the grand prix of Singapore. Others got lost in the jungles encountering rhinos and other wild life.

Jendarata was an estate in the Telok Anson area that had the most European personnel. It was a Danish system, mainly palm oil, and kept a high standard of operation. The estate was divided into several divisions, each of which had a settlement of several hundred workers (mainly families of uneducated Tamils, indentured laborers brought over from India). They lived in labor lines (rows of attached houses that had space for cooking and communal activities on a common first floor and sleeping quarters on the second floor). Palm oil or rubber was collected each day and brought to a factory for processing.

Factories and estates were managed by "planters" from overseas. This pattern gradually broke down as a "Malaysian Plan" to replace expats making the way for locals. This was the same plan that effected missionaries, only coming sooner as there were not usually the same economic factors involved and missionaries encouraged the development of local leadership.

We got to know a few of these venturesome persons while in the Telok Anson area. Later we connected with Bob and Marjorie Woods in New Zealand. Allen and Anne Awcock were good friends.

Stewardship

The ELCM inherited a history of poor stewardship. They had difficulty understanding that stewardship included all of life and thought that they could increase financial giving by simply passing rules. After years of sharing my ideas, the Diocesan Council was desperate and consented to try a new program, but they were not supportive of assigning a person to this task. Bishop Bertil Enwall of the Church of Sweden Mission did not grasp the overall concept, looked upon it as an American gimmick, and so reverted back to his state church way of operation. It became clear that the bishop was highly suspicious of Americans and reticent to accept their ideas. I served on the DC for awhile, about a year-and-a-half before going on furlough. The bishop and I were the only missionaries on the Diocesan Council at that time.

Visit to Sumatra

In April 1969 Carl Gustaf Stenback, who would become a brother in the faith to me, and I made a visit to the Batak Churches of Sumatra. We traveled extensively through the countryside and towns, hosted by the Huria Kristian Batak Protestant. The church there was alive and exciting and we were uplifted by their worship and singing. It is said that where there are two Bataks, they form a prayer fellowship, where there are three, they start a church, and where there are four, they start a choir (with four-part harmony). One of the best choirs I have ever heard was the student choir at the large Lutheran church in Medan. They gave us a private concert one Saturday afternoon, in four different languages. While there we explored the possibility of Tamil ministry, but found out that it was not viable for the ELCM. This was really the beginning of what would become a partnership in the Gospel with Carl Gustaf that would last until his untimely death in 2005.

Trouble in Kuala Lumpur

The fragile ethnic relationships, especially between the Chinese and Malays, broke down in May 1969. Singapore had come into the union in 1963 and made steady inroads politically until their departure. Elections were held and the Malay balance of power was threatened. The hatred between the two groups came to the boiling point and riots broke out, mainly in Kuala Lumpur (KL). There was mass butchering on both sides, with the Indians sometimes caught in the middle. No one knows for sure the number of deaths, but it was clearly in the thousands. During this time I took a trip to KL, coming into town when the curfew had been lifted so that people could get food. There was military about three yards apart lining both sides of the street as I came into town. Eventually things calmed down. Singapore left the union and peace prevailed.

Wider Activities

During our second term things began to snowball and accumulate on us. We had many people visiting us in Simpang Empat. This meant that most of them would be fed by us. It was not uncommon for there to be one or two extra places at our table. While this was generally stimulating for us, it took its toll on family life and budget. One month we were surprised that we had served 150 extra meals that month. Marcie served on the Missionary Executive Committee as resthouse supervisor, which meant that she would travel to the Cameron Highlands, as well as KL. I served as pastor of both the Kuala Kangsar Parish and the Teluk Anson Parish for over a year. I also served on the church's Board of Evangelism and on the Diocesan Council for a term. Plus there were other assignments, such as chaplain for retreats. All this meant that we were stretched in terms of our family life and well-being. When we went on holidays it was a real respite from those demanding days.

One of the problems we encountered occurred during monsoon season. In the evening with rains coming and flooding the low water table, cobra snakes would come right up to the doorway of our home. I kept a long bamboo pole handy and when they got too close I would whip their heads off. They were small snakes of just a few inches to two feet, but they were still poisonous.

Another figure we got to know in Telok Anson was the Raja Muda the heir to the Sultanite of Perak. His residence there made Telok Anson the second royal city we lived in. I played golf with him and he called me "Father" Vierow.

Family Activities

We would get out of Simpang Empat and Teluk Anson periodically to Ipoh, where we swam and played. The kids often had playmates who were children of missionaries in Ipoh. And we usually had a meal at the "Club" before returning home. Sometimes we stayed an extra day in the Ipoh area and I would play a round of golf with Harold Clark. We usually stayed with the Fishers, who had moved to Ipoh after language studies. Carl and I would have discussions into the night on mission strategy. Carl was a real southern gentleman who had good family times with his wife Miriam and his four children. We have remained close over the years.

Once in a while we would go to "Golden Sands," the Baptist place in Port Dickson, where we would have missionary meetings. I remember being chaplain one year and having talks using the characters of "Peanuts" which I drew and put on the fleece board. These were times when we conversed about various things related to mission, but also had fun times together. Meals were shared in common and sporting activities were organized. Since we we were "on the fringe", off the beaten path, and with "the other church," we soaked in these times.

But perhaps the most relaxing times were in the Cameron Highlands at the Lutheran Bungalow. This was a place 5,000 feet up over the town of Tanah Rata, a town two miles distant. Here were accommodations for several families with fireplaces and cool weather. Often several of our friends would be there so Hiltje and Dane would have playmates, and in the evening Marcie and I would play table games late into the night with friends. I usually took Hiltje and Dane hiking in the jungle during these outings. We would explore the flora and fauna. The jungle was real, but fairly close to civilization, so we always found our way back and stuck to pathways made by others -- except on one occasion when we got lost and ended up getting out through an aboriginal village.

Those were the times when the country was still largely virgin jungle and one could walk in the jungle and not see the sun. The canopy was perhaps 70 feet high. There was vegetation everywhere, so when we got off the path, we were certainly aware of it. We would search for "pouchies," cold weather centipedes in a shell that hung out in mossy areas, or "monkey pods," which were a special kind of vine plant whose cup actually caught bugs and digested them. Of course there was play equipment right on the property and visits to various attractions in the area. And the flowers were always in bloom. Among other things, fern trees spread overhead and tapirs roamed below. They were fairly docile, but that was not so for the tigers. At one juncture we had to be careful of the children because tiger paws were seen on the cars. When night came, we actually looked out the window and saw a tiger climbing over the cars, looking for prey.

There were some short walks to waterfalls in the area, which we would take as a family. The best one was just a short distance up from the hog farm. The golf course was just below the bungalow, and I would have a couple of rounds there, especially if Clarks were at the Baptist bungalow. Once we came across the King playing a round of golf. The UMNO (political coalition) bungalow was right below ours. Tunkgu Abdul Rahman, the father of the country, was frequently there. Services were held every Sunday at the local Anglican Church. A movie was available several nights a week at the local theatre run by those who were associated with the British unit in town, where they played "God Save the Queen" each night. When we left the Cameron Highlands, we were usually rested and happy, ready to return to work.

Problems

Hiltje and Dane continued to develop, and early on their mother home schooled them. We had a special room set aside for this. This worked for awhile, but having mom teach them did not work in the long run. Part of the time they went to "Auntie Anne's" school, a part-time school taught by Anne Åwcock, wife of Alan and dear friends of ours. But the Awcocks left for home leave.

As the months passed, the brunt of the burden seemed to fall heaviest on Marcie. When I pleaded with her to join me on a trip to Ipoh to get away, she declined saying there was too much to do and she would stay back. Eventually she went to stay with Ute Volp, a German doctor and friend, for a few days. Dr. Volp wrote that Marcie was suffering from extreme mental exhaustion and needed some rest. She remained there for a few days. But when she returned, it was with a different attitude.

She seemed to hold me directly responsible for her situation. But we had conferred about going to Simpang Empat, knowing the difficulties. She felt we should go, but in the end it was too much for her. Solbergs, our good friends who were at Bethany Home, left for home leave.

Children's Activities

We tried to read to Hiltje and Dane regularly at bedtime. Marcie did this much more than I because I was gone a good deal of the time. I regretted relegating so much of the childcare to her as I found out later when discussing their perceptions. We read all the Narnia stories.

During Advent season we had our own form of the Advent wreath with places for candles for each day of the season. This was one way that we could communicate the anticipation of the birth of Christ.

It was during this time that I conceived of the idea of writing a children's story for the kids and illustrate it. "The Tiger, the Pigs and the Elephant" story evolved. The kids enjoyed the project and it was approved for publication in Sweden, but I did not have time to separate the various colors for printing.

Hiltje and Dane had several playmates from the community and the home for epileptic children behind us. It was always a joy to go to Ipoh for a swim or playtimes with the Fisher clan.

We made the celebration of special occasions like birthdays a big deal, especially for the children. When Dane was young he signed his name Dane4, as if his age was part of his name. So on his fourth birthday we made a cake into a big four. We continued the tradition up until he was ten. When he turned five we had a very special "pirates" party, complete with swash-buckling swords, hats and games to match.

The whole party took place aboard a large boat (complete with crew) of the marine patrol of lower Perak in Teluk Anson. The boat went up and down the Perak River as about 15 people (most of them under eight) sang Happy Birthday to him. There was his Malay neighbor, a boy from the Tamil labor lines, a couple of town kids, a couple of kids that were expats, and children of estate staff. Hiltje and a few girls were present. Other birthdays for both children were sometimes celebrated in the Cameron Highlands with missionary children.

Hiltje's Schooling

We had spent long hours in discussion and still didn't have a solution to the problem of Hiltje's schooling. It did not work out having Mom do it; the time spent with Auntie Anne was helpful but cut short by their home leave. In spite of getting special permission for Hiltje to attend the local school, the use of Malay and the style of teaching was clearly not providing her a good education and fifty students to a class was questionable. We really struggled and finally concluded that we would try sending her away to boarding school. We had three options: the International School in Singapore, the Overseas Missionary Fellowship School in the Cameron Highlands, or a British school on Penang Hill.

Singapore seemed too far away, so it was a toss-up between the OMF School and Penang. We really struggled with what should be done. Marcie felt that a British school in Penang would be better so we proceeded to enroll Hiltje there. The six months spent there were difficult months. I remember picking up Hiltje at the Ipoh airport. She was a brave seven-year-old who had a desire to do well in school.

News from the States was not good. My sister was getting a divorce from her husband and leaving the four children. My parents had taken an extra mortgage on their home to help their son-in-law purchase a local bar, and now, as they were coming into an age when finances were crucial to the their well-being, they were in danger of losing their home. I spoke with the bishop about the problem and he helped me decide to go back six months early.

Second Furlough

As a family we came in January 1970 from a hot tropical climate to the dead of winter in Minnesota. It was quite a shock. I climbed in bed, put tons of blankets on me; I was physically, mentally, and emotionally drained. It took us some days to recover. But we were home again at my parent's house. We were able to get the house situation dealt with in an agreeable fashion, and we enjoyed the family time together.

The ensuing months were a gift of relaxation and recuperation of family time together and reconnecting to our home base of supporting congregations. We were housed in a duplex at 3854 South Elliot Avenue in Minneapolis. This was a missionary residence, fully furnished, with space for Hiltje and Dane to play and the fine missionary family of Paul and Loi Setterholm as neighbors. The kids were enrolled in a Lutheran parochial school that gave a discount to missionaries.

Gustavus Adolpus College

That summer and autumn in Minnesota were important to us, for we were able to be together as a family, to enjoy friends and life in America. I was assigned as "Missionary in Residence" at Gustavus

Adolpus College in St. Peter, Minnesota. My role was one of teaching (Church History, South East Asia Studies), relating to the community, and generally raising mission awareness.

We moved into a marvelous old farm house four miles west of town, owned by Russell and Myrtle, who lived just across the road, but were gone in Arizona for the winter. There was an old barn with other farm buildings and lots of space for us to play and wander about. Just after we arrived, Russell and Myrtle were harvesting corn and said we were free to take what we wanted. With freezer provided, we proceeded to put up corn in the freezer that lasted until we left.

Hiltje and Dane were enrolled in the local school. Dane had to take an exam because his birthday was a few days short of the age limit, but we knew him to be ready. It took him a while to adjust, but both had a good experience there. I recall once when school was let out early because a snowstorm was imminent, but the kids were nestled safely in the barn next to the house. We learned again that snowstorms in Minnesota need to be given their due and we just holed up for a day or two when we were "snowed in." Once, we ended up leaving the car on the road in the middle of a snow bank since we could not even tell where the road was. I had a tow truck recover it from the middle of the road the next day. When we took it to the garage, it was one big ice block that needed to be thawed out.

There is a special beauty about life after the storm when all is calm, snowdrifts carve out lines of beauty, and there is crystalline ice on the trees. Your family is all nice and cozy and you have a day away from any schedule. It is a gift to be enjoyed to the fullest.

The time at Gustavus Adolphus College was a difficult, but welcome change of pace. Difficult because I was not prepared for what I would find in college students in 1970. I went through college at a time when we were content to study and have traditional activities. But by 1970 students were ready to get involved, take over campus if necessary, and speak out on issues that were vital to them. Women's lib was in full force, the "pill" was used around campus, and peace symbols were everywhere.

I confess I went into the classroom of 70 students with fear and trepidation. By the end of term I felt OK with the whole thing, but it was quite an adjustment. I took painting once a week and enjoyed getting in touch with my more creative side. I painted a piece that had three panels depicting with symbols the struggle of the times, including mini skirts, peace symbols, the pill, black power, a shotgun, and Uncle Sam upside down. I left this piece with Esther Schmidt, who named it "My Country 'Tis of Thee" and entered it into the Minnesota State Fair art show. To my surprise it was accepted and hung in the art display at State Fair that year.

There were many additional activities around campus, preaching in chapel, relating to groups, dialoging with profs, and attending special events, including an emphasis on mission. I taught a course in January term on Southeast Asia studies. During our mission emphasis, I brought Subamma, a sharp, independent, single, high-caste woman from Andhra Pradesh in India. Dr. Sue was finishing up studies at Fuller School of World Mission for her doctorate and was a big hit with faculty and students. We developed a close relationship during that time. Sue has served well in ministry to the poor, especially women. She developed an Ashram program for the women of the United Lutheran Church in India.

The time we spent at St. Peter was a blessed time that God provided because he knew we needed that time to re-energize ourselves. Marcie and I began to build an open and honest relationship. Hiltje and Dane settled into school. Halloween and Thanksgiving took on new meaning for them. We all enjoyed the picturesque autumn on our rented farm. How we would have liked to prolong those last days of colored leaves and harvest time -- the winter snow as it drifted and blew-- bedazzled us as we saw it so rarely.

I enjoyed our sojourn at St. Peter. Getting to know profs was regenerating for me and I was able to connect with Dick Elvee, an old seminary buddy who was chaplain. I particularly liked the more relaxed atmosphere of living in the rural area, yet close to the town of St. Peter and life on a college campus. While there, we were members of First Lutheran Church where Herb Chilstrom, who was to become head bishop of the Evangelical Lutheran Church in America, served as pastor.

When we left the college, I felt refreshed, ready to make a significant contribution in Malaysia.

8. CONCLUSION OF OVERSEAS SERVICE

The first two terms I had been heavily involved working in outreach among estate laborers. This was essential for the early stages of missionary work, and I believe we followed a model that was effective. I shifted gears during my third term when I had been assigned to develop a training program for the lay persons in congregations. If the church was to grow, then people would have to be trained to do the many tasks that were necessary to care for membersto grow and reach out effectively. As missionaries our time was definitely limited. Local leaders needed to be trained.

Africa

I was eager to get back to Malaysia and the work there. I would be stationed in Kuala Lumpur area where Hiltje and Dane would have adequate schooling. En route back to Malaysia we stopped in Nigeria and Tanzania, where they had active and successful lay training programs working within the structures of the national churches. We arrived in Lagos, capital city of war-torn Nigeria. For some reason they did not have our hotel reservations. We ended up scrounging around and finally found a remote mosquito- infested Muslim guesthouse. I stayed up that night fanning the kids and Marcie so that mosquitoes would not bite them too badly. The next day we left for the facility where the training was located, which was a welcomed site after Lagos. Tanzania with a program in extension was more geared to our needs, and we enjoyed our time there with the Stan and Marie Benson.

One trip I made with Stan Benson was particularly notable. It was an overnight trip, a 50-mile trek off the beaten path, to a remote village of Masai people. They were a nomadic tribe that had settled into a community out in the remote areas of the Tanzanian savannah, far removed from the mainstream accessible by driving on remote, dry riverbeds. They were known for their unique lifestyle that included the drinking of blood from their cow herds and men dressed with tunics, beads around their necks, and reddish hair matted with mud from the soil. Dancing, these men (tall by Tanzanian standards) would leap high into the air. With tunics and spears, they made quite a sight to the casual observer. Shepherding their cattle was their main activity.

We had an Indian along (East Indians provided a good deal of the trading in rural areas). We drove on a seemingly uncharted path through the bush country with ostriches running alongside us and occasionally we came across a young warrior who was tending his herd of cattle. Along the way the car, a Landrover, broke down. While they were repairing the axle at a settlement, I sat down on the veranda of a mud house in the only chair that seemed available. After taking in the scenery, I settled into reading the Bible I had along. Before long I noticed that there was someone behind me looking at the Bible. I said to him, "Do you speak English?" "Yes, a little," came the reply. He read part of the Bible, and I asked him what his name was. This young man, dressed as a Masai warrior with spear and tunic in hand, responded by saying, "My name is Johnson." I nearly fell off the chair. Apparently a missionary by the name of Johnson had baptized him, and he took that name as his own.

When we arrived in the settlement of Masai, there was a stir in the community. It seems a herd of elephants had taken to using the watering tank that they had for watering their cattle and were threatening to take over that facility. Cattle are vital to the well being of the Masai, but elephants were protected by the game reserve people. The night before certain young warriors had taken upon themselves the task of defending the Masai rights to the tank by attacking the herd of elephants. They did this with a few machetes. A few of them hid in the bushes while others created a ruckus to scare the elephants that then ran in the direction of the young men hiding in the bushes. As the elephants passed by, they attacked them with their machetes slashing at the back of the huge beasts' legs and thus causing them to fall down helpless. They were careful not to take the valuable tusks for the authorities would be along soon. The young warriors had proven themselves as brave men and were held in honor by the tribe.

The local health clinic had indicated that the young men had not had a casualty among them. The next morning when we had a communion service I could not follow the Swahili, but surely there was an element of thanksgiving for their safety and a relief that their herd was now safe from these formidable intruders.

Back at the training center, thanks to Stan and Marie Benson, we feasted on wild game and locally grown berries before we departed for Malaysia.

Assignment - Third Term – Lay Training

We returned to our beloved Malaysia. My main task during our third term was to design, set up, and run a lay training program for the ELCMS. In conversation with Ralph Winter and his experience in establishing at Theological Education Program by Extension in Latin America, I had discovered a sound model for a solution to the ELCMS need. We could establish a program that had programmed learning, an easy-to-follow lesson plan, and training in various centers around the country. It was clear that a program in extension was necessary as potential students were scattered throughout the Malay Peninsula and Singapore. Rather than have the students come to a central place for their training as was the case for so much training, TEE allowed us to bring the training to the students. This was much more workable than the traditional system. I was able to provide a workshop by Peter Sentner from Central America for key leaders. Soon we were producing our own materials and enrolling students around the country and Singapore.

Resource persons were primarily pastors or evangelists who could serve on a part-time basis in their respective areas. "Programmed" materials were designed in Tamil and English so that students could get immediate feedback on the weekly materials before coming to "class," which included a discussion on the topic of the week, a worship experience, and an introductory presentation on the next topic. We held occasional regional and national gatherings for all, and each 12-session term had a teacher's training session held in Kuala Lumpur.

Esprit de corps was high as we launched the program. As director I was kept busy training, preparing materials, organizing special events, and visiting each of the 15 sites once per term. I was ably assisted by Carl Gustaf Stenback in Penang and a core staff at headquarters in KL including translators. It was quite a chore getting lessons prepared and tested, teachers enlisted and trained, and then teaching some and traveling about the country visiting each site. But it was a program that fully involved 15 per cent of the laypersons of the church and I felt well worth the effort.

I had known most of the teachers over the years and worked with them. One was a retired Tamil schoolteacher, Devadasson, from Ipoh, who in spite of an asthmatic condition traveled by bus to rural areas to hold classes.

The plan was to have two years of general training with Biblical, historical and doctrinal content for everyone, and then branch out into specializations, like leading worship, teaching, evangelism, and youth ministry. The potential for extended ministry was amazing and our people began to see the possibilities. Students were enthusiastic and embraced the plan. Teachers saw the potential for extending ministry. This presented a threat to those in authority. I had prepared every aspect of the program, but I had failed to educate adequately the ELCMS leadership. Somehow, I thought the bishop and other leaders would advocate for the program, but I found out otherwise. I recall a confrontation with Bishop Envall in his office when I stated that I had given my all to the church and pleaded with him that he trust me to do the work assigned to me. It was clear that this would not be the case. The rug was pulled out from under the program by taking away the specializations. When I left, the program was dropped and the ELCMS has continued to struggle to this very day. Many of the laity have left the Lutheran Church for more positive experiences.

Sunday Evenings

An aspect of ministry that I enjoyed was the Sunday Evening English service at the church in Brickfields. A number of youth had wanted an English service for some time, and with me there it seemed like a natural assignment. There were older adults that also attended, but by and large those who came were young people. They were enthusiastic and excited about life, and I tried to bring them messages that were interesting and on topics that they had investment in. S. G. Achariam was pastor-in-charge, and we had a good working relationship. There were a number of youth events that I participated in regularly, like the retreat.

One of the things I remember about that time was that I coached a makeshift basketball team. We had a court connected to the church, and the boys were more enthusiastic than skilled. I still hear words of appreciation for these ministries when I return to Malaysia.

Kuala Lumpur

Over the next five years we would live in three different homes in Petaling Jaya (PJ), at that time a developing town near KL where the churches had work and key persons lived. The first home was owned by the Southern Baptists and was available for a short time. I remember it as the place where Dane and I built his go-cart. We had purchased a kit in the states, but it still took work. We tried it out on the street we lived on, actually launching it in our driveway and down the road near our new residence. Later we carried it on top of the car to the Cameron Highlands and took it down the hill with its long winding road from the Lutheran bungalow. It was quite a sight: Dane in the go cart and I perched on top of the car trying to film the event and go ahead of the cart. We had a good time with friends and family.

The second house we lived in for the remainder of our second term was perched on the side of a hill. It provided a "home" where we could function effectively. Dane and Hiltje were bussed by van with other missionary kids to the "ISKL," the International School in Kuala Lumpur. The school provided a good base for the kids and many happy occasions. At home we had the Malay playhouse that we had constructed in Simpang

Empat placed in the yard, shared by a turkey and duck that were good pets. Hiltje and Dane would have friends over, and Hiltje was good at directing activities, like a circus on the veranda.

Dane's Accident

At home Dane had a nasty accident on the occasion of Hiltje's tenth birthday. It was a bowling party and Dane had to leave early to make it next door to his swimming lesson. He ran into a glass pane that, when I got to him just after the impact, held a huge glass "V" ready to fall, which would have surely severed him. That night I wrote the following poem:

A Birthday Celebration

A joyous time! A birthday celebration!

Suddenly – the sound of glass, a smash!
    and all joy and laughter, thoughts and emotions
    are shattered to bits
    like the glass
    as the name -- "Dane" -- is sounded!
My God! . . . . I ran to find
    the scattered glass
    the stunned crowd
    and my son . . .
        a mass of cut and bleeding flesh
        (the dreams of a father in limbo)

A car, a car! Oh God, a car!
    a kingdom for . . .
But God was summoned and present
    (need I have worried more?)
    a friend, by chance (?), a car
    and God was also here -- to guide
        the boy -- confused but brave

the doctor -- young, but a father himself
      who knew the turmoil, the depth of love
the parents -- in prayerful anxiety

Each to discover -- that God's acts are gracious
    beyond measure,
    every artery, nerve, and vital organ was spared
    to give to God the glory.

Then a joy and thanksgiving beyond all knowing
    and expression,
    and a cut up, bloodied and bandaged little boy --
    a living example of God's miracle.

We were grateful that he only had cuts over his body and a leg that seemed close to being cut in half was spared. After several weeks he recovered fully. On another occasion he had a bone infection in his left arm, which was painful and undetectable until x-rays revealed that half his femur had been eaten away.

Moving to "KL"

Moving to the "KL" area allowed us into a different kind of life style as well as atmosphere in the churches. We were definitely part of the Lutheran/American missionary group and the ISKL parents. We focused on our relationship within the Tamil (ELCMS--Evangelical Lutheran Church of Malaysia and Singapore) Church though we still had contact with many of the leaders of the LCMS (Lutheran Church of Malaysia and Singapore). We were able to go to more cultural events and watch TV. (The Malaysia TV industry was beyond its infancy stage and we caught some of the old reruns from the USA like "All in the Family" and "Gilligan's Island.")

Life in the churches was different also. We were now part of a more "sophisticated" group, and there was definitely politics in the church. This was perhaps most evident during the annual General Assembly of the ELCMS when discussions would go on for long periods. The Tamil tendency toward litigation and long talk was very much a part of life. On one occasion it took several hours to deal with the question: "Was the meeting properly convened?" I stayed out of these, of course, but they certainly wore down one's ability to stay cool.

Over the years I served on the outreach committee, youth planning, stewardship team (the basic tenet that "all of life is a gift of God and that all belongs to God and is to be used as God wills" was a concept, which that very few grasped when it came to church life). It did not help, of course, that the Church of Sweden Mission pumped in big amounts of money. The ELCMS had somehow gotten the "State" Church mentality. In spite of our efforts, the dependence of the local church on the mission was apparent and had a negative effect on the church's ability to be self-supporting.

A Lesson on Communication

Back in the 60s there were no food establishment chains from the United States doing business in Malaysia. The first to come was the A&W in Petaling Jaya. It did not catch on like they had hoped until they asked the Malay community why they were not frequenting the new venture. The A & W was told that a Malay person would never come because they sold "hamburgers" and ham was a forbidden food for Muslims.

Further, they said, "You sell beer. We cannot drink beer either, and you advertise that you have root beer for sale."

Communicating with Congregations

Over the years in the mission field I corresponded with a lot of people. There was the need to communicate with supporting congregations. They were:

> Atonement Lutheran in Bloomington, Minnesota
> St. Mark's Lutheran in North St. Paul, Minnesota
> St. Mark's Lutheran Church in Waukesha, Wisconsin
> St. Paul's Lutheran in Davenport, Iowa

Trinity Lutheran in Lebanon, Indiana
The Lutheran Congregation in Lihue, Kauai, Hawaii
Wooddale Lutheran in St. Louis Park, Minnesota

During furlough we would try to visit each of these congregations, but when in the field we primarily used a newsletter I named "Malaysian Memoirs." In the 19 plus years I served as a missionary, there were 58 issues (ranging from one page to a booklet). There were 250 on the mailing list, and several congregations sent them to the members. Several of the issues were published, including one in Swedish.

In addition I wrote a number of daily devotionals. I wrote regularly for "The Word in Season" (the devotional I had sent out during seminary days), booklets and articles for church magazines. I felt that communication with church members was important and took the responsibility seriously. Today there are all sorts of avenues of communication open the world over, but back in those days we were pretty limited.

A Special Perk

Before we left Malaysia to go back to the States for furlough we found that Northwest Airlines had a special promotion. For just $10 we could fly across America first class. Dane was fascinated with air travel and we were able to book a flight to California on his ninth birthday on a new 747. We sat in the very front of the plane and back in those days (1973) we could move about freely. Dane not only got a special set of wings, but also was invited into the cockpit for a personalized tour by the captain. He was on cloud nine! Later in life he would become a recreational pilot.

9. THE SHAPING OF A MISSIOLOGIST

Fuller School of World Mission

When I weighed the ministry I was allowed to have and the knowledge and talents I brought to ministry, I came to the conclusion that I could no longer be effective under the leadership of the ELCM. As long as Bishop Envall, with his mistrust of Americans, was there, I could be more productive elsewhere.

Pastor Gideon Chang gave me my Chinese name, Wei Lou Ming, when I first arrived in Malaya. Later to be bishop of the LCMS, he was acting bishop when I left Malaysia at the conclusion of our third term in August 1973. After stops in Sweden to visit missionary friends, the Netherlands to visit IFYE families, and our families in the Midwest, we moved to Pasadena, California, where I attended the Fuller School of World Mission.

Missiology is the study of the cross-cultural communication of the Gospel. A missiologist is one who practices an interdisciplinary study, using theology, history, anthropology, sociology, linguistics, ecclesiology and other disciplines that assist in understanding the complexities of cross cultural communication of the Gospel in developing strategies for mission outreach.

The School of World Mission was out in the forefront of missiological thought, having been founded by Donald McGavran a few years earlier.

Much of what was getting attention in missiology was coming from Pasadena. If I were going to be prepared to take on new tasks in Malaysia, this would be the best place to attend, so our furlough was largely spent attending classes for the fall term.

The classroom was exciting as courses were taught by Donald McGavran, Alan Tippett, Ralph Winter, Art Glasser, Charles Kraft, and Peter Wagner. Equally stimulating were classmates who had a wide variety of overseas experience, including key national church leaders from Africa, Asia, and Latin America. Discussions were filled with wisdom and the Holy Spirit. I was affirmed in the basic approach I had been using as a missionary and the strategy used. I was among people who were as passionate for the Gospel as I was.

I left the end of December to journey back to Malaysia for a fourth term. Our visa was approved only after I indicated that I would be leaving after 22 months. I had already stayed longer than allowed for expatriates.

Hiltje, Marcie, Dane and I at home in Petaling Jaya 1974

PJ – Church Growth – Teaching

We settled into our new quarters, which was just a stone's throw away from fellow missionary Dick Zimmerman's house and what was, then, the new Petaling Jaya. The kids had playmates nearby and by now felt comfortable in the International School.

After attending Fuller and in conference with Malaysian folk, it was decided that I would set up a national church growth office, assisting a variety of denominations with their outreach plans. The old Lutheran Bible Institute had enough space, so I got a secretary and we set up shop.

Knowing the situation in Malaysia, it did not take me long to get going. I set up a governing council and was meeting with representatives of some of the more than 15 agencies I related to. The LCMS, Baptists, Pentecostals, Navigators, Campus Crusade, Friends, Presbyterians, and Methodists were all involved.

Part of church growth was the need for accurate information. I spent part of my time gathering information on the various churches, demographic and population statistics for Malaysia. Graphs of interest with comparative growth of the Christian community were made. Eventually this was all placed in a book and published by Glad Sounds with the title of "Malaysian Christian Handbook." I also wrote a "profile" of Malaysia and the "Status of Christianity" for background material for the Lausanne Conference on World Evangelization.

The main thrust, however, was getting the various churches and agencies to develop their own strategies for church growth. I organized a workshop with Donald McGavran at Port Dickson, which had a large group of enthusiastic Christian leaders. The "esprit de corps" was high and the overall strategies were advanced. This was followed up by invitations from a variety of churches and organizations. Rarely does a Lutheran get to preach in Baptist churches and at the training center for the Assemblies of God. My schedule was filled with such invitations.

A good deal of my time during those months was devoted to a preaching and teaching ministry. For the LCMS I led monthly English Services at Taman Midah, a suburb of KL. This was a new outreach ministry that grew rapidly. I also taught lay training classes at Setapek. The 15 or so students there were among the most dedicated and enthusiastic I have ever had the privilege of teaching

It was during this time that I was very much attracted to the Baptist church. I liked their enthusiasm and plans for outreach, but I could not resolve my uneasiness with their decision theology. It seemed to smack of work-righteousness, something that Luther was very much aware of and spoke out against.

I remember a conversation I had with my Dutch father on a visit to Friesland during his last years. He was active and served for many years in the Reformed Church. He was worried, almost obsessed, with knowing that his life was near the end and he would be found spiritual lacking. The idea that you don't earn your way into the Kingdom of God, but that it is a free gift of God's grace made possible by the cross, was liberating for him. Still, he struggled with this until his dying day.

How grateful I am for a solid theological foundation that forms and informs me daily. There is some flexibility in applying this, but it is the Word of God that is the final authority.

There was an alternative form of theological education that developed in Klang. This was a self-supporting community run by a Presbyterian missionary by the name of Day. I taught evening and daytime classes in Bible, church growth, and history and filled in for Day when he went on furlough. Several young people were trained and became effective workers. They lived in the community, took classes in the morning, worked in the afternoon, and studied at night. Weekends were devoted to work in churches.

Theological Training

There was a growing dissatisfaction with existing arrangements and programs for training for full time ministry. There was the desire of all churches for the training of laity and continuing education of present church workers. But it became clear that it was necessary to do more research, so I undertook the gathering of information and the compiling of a survey and analysis of theological training in Malaysia.

I interviewed over 40 church leaders and educators. The paper was over 70 pages in length but provided a basis for discussion.

I had attended a conference in Hong Kong on theological education in Asia and visited leaders of the church leaders of East Malaysia. I also organized a workshop on Theological Education by Extension. In June 1974 we gathered church leaders from a variety of churches to discuss the paper I had written. My paper focused on the current theological education, the need for a distinct Malaysia setting and call to plan cooperatively. It was perhaps one of the most diverse representations of churches up to that time. Discussion was animated and a variety of opinions was voiced. A continuing group met and eventually two strands of interest were pursued. One was a group interested in providing training for workers in Chinese and English and conservative in orientation. Classes were held at first at the old Lutheran Bible Institute in PJ. The other group was made up of those churches that belonged to the Malaysian Christian Council and were already cooperating at Trinity College in Singapore. The idea was to establish a Malaysian setting for theological education.

I felt good that my paper had started the discussion and decision-making. My position allowed me the freedom to be able to function in this way. It was quite a change from my days with the ELCMS.

As I saw it, I had acted as catalyst and resource person in the areas of theological education and church growth for the wider church. Facilitating these two concerns was my goal and could be done by an expatriate who was on the way out but still with ability to contribute to the overall mission advancement. I was grateful to God for the manner in which things developed in these areas.

The survey I made in 1974 indicated the need and desire to establish training in and for the Malaysian setting. There were at least five reasons for this:
1. Political pressures made it evident that a Malaysian training was preferable.
2. There is a strong nationalistic spirit among church leaders.

3. Students training elsewhere had difficulty understanding and ministering in Malaysia. There was a need to "contextualize" training.
4. There was little or no contact between churches and those who were being trained.
5. A need was evident for a broader training, not just for ministerial students, and for more flexible patterns.

After our initial meeting, a series of consultations was held and a plan for the formation of a new seminary "Seminari Theologi Malaysia" came into being. A cooperative effort of Anglicans, Lutherans, Methodists, and Presbyterians, this school has made a substantial contribution to Malaysian society.

We managed to get a trip/vacation in to East Malaysia. We visited the Clarks in Sarawak and played our last round of golf together. (Harold Clark died suddenly after going jogging shortly thereafter.) Through contacts with various mission agencies, we were able to visit some of the people of Sabah, including the Dusans of North Borneo fame and hear the amazing story of faith in establishing a church among them. The Lutheran Church there has done outstanding work. We were inspired by the trip and getting to know Christian workers. The information I received was helpful.

It was during this time that we visited Singapore as well. I began the process of exploring a combination job of lecturing at Singapore Bible College and Trinity Theological College upon return from furlough, which would have been in 1976. I found that both institutions were interested in making this happen.

Concluding Overseas Service

During my years as a missionary I threw myself into the demands of being an effective missionary: not only the reading of journals and learning language, but the cultural issues, recent trends in mission, Bible, religion and the particularities of Malaysian life and society (learning patterns of life, how each part of society fit into a whole, the proper ways of addressing and acknowledging persons, the sheer logistics of getting about to remote places by car, walking, bus, bicycle or river launch; the flow of the working day; the transportation system; and family patterns); all of these things were new to me and even though I was trained well as a pastor and missionary, had to be learned. There was sermon (in Tamil) preparation, worship services at several places, prayers with families, supervision of schools, of evangelist, meeting with youth leaders and council: there was service on the boards of the national church, planning for youth assembly. It was all very exciting and interesting. Then there was the need to devote time to family and plan for time away.

I entered these tasks with joy and enthusiasm, eager to learn and grow in understanding. Sometimes with sheer abandon, throwing caution to the winds, I would do whatever necessary to complete the task. It was during this time that Marcie and I had discussion on opportunities and the unique quality and character of the events before us. I felt an urgent need to make the best of each opportunity.

I left Malaysia on November 15, 1975, when I was 40 years old. My visa ran out at midnight. I believed there was no greater joy than serving as a missionary of our Lord Jesus Christ, and no better place than Asia to fulfill it.

End of 1975

We visited families and four supporting congregations on successive Sundays, purchased a car and drove to California, and had terrific seats for the Rose Bowl Parade in Pasadena. For housing we were able to get quarters at what would become the US Center for World Mission. Hiltje and Dane were admitted into the local school system, which was quite a let down after the International School of Kuala Lumpur.

The Division of World Mission and Ecumenism (DWME) of the Lutheran Church in America had agreed to allow me two terms at Fuller School of World Mission. Art Glasser was assigned as my advisor and I quickly got into a schedule of reading, taking classes, preparing for comprehensive exams, and building on the research I had done to prepare a dissertation appropriate to a doctorate degree in Missiology offered at that time. This would be good for my position in Singapore, I thought.

It was a joy to take classes again from Ralph Winter, one of the great mission thinkers of our time.

Dr. Glasser was a great advisor and took me through all the necessary steps, which included editing 15 pages of my dissertation as I frantically prepared it each day, so that I could meet the deadline for submission of the manuscript in time. Marcie spent much time typing up the draft. Dr. Donald A. McGavran and Dr. C. Peter Wagner were the other members of my committee. The day of my defense was a day filled with affirmation of my ministry in mission. I was humbled and grateful for the opportunity that Fuller School of World Mission provided me.

But there loomed a much bigger problem on the horizon that had the potential to bring all that I had been working for to naught.

10. TRANSITION

In Limbo 1976

My parents came out and witnessed my getting the degree in June 1976. It should have been a day of joy, yet for me it was very sad for Marcie was convinced our marriage should end. She decided to stay in California to continue counseling and take time for herself while I went back to the Midwest with the kids.

Under the circumstances, we had a good trip back, stopping to camp under the giant redwoods of northern California, at Crater Lake, at Livingston, Montana (where we visited and stayed with members of the congregation I had served there in 1960). Getting in touch with God's great creation, having time with the kids and camping along the way gave me a sense of God's caring, which would become vital for the storm ahead.

As a missionary with an advanced degree, I was posted as "Missionary in Residence" to Northwestern and Luther Theological Seminaries. (They were going through what was known as "maximal functional unification" at the time, which led to the merger of the two schools.) We were given residence at a huge old house on campus, centrally located. We moved in and I began to prepare for teaching. The kids were admitted into the school nearby. Marcie and I immediately went into counseling: she for the purpose of proceeding with a divorce, and I for the purpose of saving a marriage.

The next few weeks were a nightmare.

Colleagues at Seminary

My time at Northwestern Lutheran and Luther Theological Seminaries was difficult due to my marital situation, but reassuring that I had something to contribute. I was, under the circumstances, somewhat intimidated by the intellectual giants who surrounded me. One of them was Paul Martinson, who was given the impossible task of teaching mission to the multitude of Luther students. He was understanding and affirming as I team-taught with him and related to mission concerns.

At Northwestern I was asked to teach a course in evangelism, since a group of students coming from internship had asked for it. (There was nothing in the curriculum.) So I designed a course that involved personal witnessing (a sharing of their personal faith stories) as well as book learning. It was a stretch for some in the class, but I think it introduced an experience that prepared them for the parish.

As I moved through the year, Professor Doris Flesner's struggle with depression became apparent. I offered to help, and we team-taught a course in ecumenism. I was delighted to contribute in this way. It was clear that the emphasis in mission, so prevalent in my time as a student, was missing. There were several of us missionary types who were concerned enough to act.

After my year at the seminary, I got a position as mission coordinator for the region. In essence it was like being a deployed staff member of the Division of World Mission of the LCA, a position created for me to transition.

I searched for a system and school that would best serve Dane, and we ended up in Plymouth at the junior high school. Marcie moved in the area and Hiltje entered high school.

When the divorce was finalized toward the end of 1977, there was a great sense of relief, as if a heavy burden had been lifted and life could begin again. We each went our separate ways.

The next two years were filled with adjusting to life as a single parent and doing the work of visiting various synods of the church in the upper midwest and central Canada.

A Holy State

I believe that marriage is a holy state. And I certainly was not going to put asunder what God had joined together, though over the years I did my share of contributing to a deteriorating relationship. After all, I was a clergy person and a missionary besides. Somehow, I thought, God would keep things together -- as if I had an inoculation to protect me from divorce when I was ordained and a booster when I was commissioned a missionary.

Ours was a whirlwind courtship. I was to leave for overseas, so we didn't have a lot of time to "waste." Nor did we seem to have time to delve into the past, explore our basic personalities, or allow time to raise and answer pertinent questions. No time, really, for doubts. When doubts did come, I quickly dismissed them, thinking they must be "hangovers" from bachelorhood. Our motto seemed to be "let's get on with the business at hand."

An Instrument of Service

That business was to be missionaries. What a fantastic life awaited us! A whole lifetime squeezed into 15 unusual, challenging, fulfilling years. Two energetic, but immature persons laboring together, excited about their part in the Lord's ministry – growing and sharing together, experiencing God's direction and grace.

Fifteen years brought many shared experiences: fighting armies of cockroaches, traveling around the globe, hiking through the jungle, experiencing tropical illness, living in 15 different homes, making countless friends, and being at the birth of two lovely children.

Marriage for us had been an instrument for service. I failed to realize that the instrument must be cared for if it was going to be of service. I neglected to cultivate the kind of communication that Marcie needed to nourish our relationship. Our relationship had become subordinate to doing our missionary work. God blessed our work in many ways. But God did not want me to become a workaholic. I had a passion to be a good missionary and a sense of urgency to get the task done. I felt that Marcie shared that passion, at least to begin with, as she tried desperately to fill the various roles with an overwhelming sense of servanthood. In the process we lost touch with one another. Being missionaries did not make us immune to the pitfalls of intense living.

Yet we had 15 years of service that were fruitful as well as diverse, meaningful as well as eventful, greatly satisfying as well as stimulating. There had been significant spiritual growth and (I thought) comfortable family life. These were years given by God to us together for service. For that I rejoice.

When the divorce came, I was crushed. Nothing I could do seemed to matter. Life went into a tailspin for a while, though a close relationship with God and responsibility for the children kept me going.

Another Crisis

In the meantime, another crisis was surfacing that was to be just as traumatic for me as the breakup of my marriage. As unprepared as I was for the divorce, I was even less prepared for this. There was a strong threat of another kind of divorce – this one from the church!

Because of my marital situation, it seemed like the church was also trying to divorce me. As I ended my missionary service and looked for a call in North America, the response I received from the leaders of the church was almost devastating. My bishop was supportive of me as a person but held out little hope for a possible call. I was told by him and others that there was a lot of stereotyped ideas about divorced persons, especially clergy, and it would be difficult, if not impossible, to get a call to a congregation.

"Where is justice?" I questioned as I struggled with this new reality in dealing with the hierarchy of the church. For in their hands lay the key to a call. "Where is justice?" I was angry. I had just been through a divorce not of my choosing, and now it seemed like I was going through another, also not of my choosing. I was determined to "hang in there."

I had completed 19 years of dedicated and fruitful ministry in missionary service. Many of those years were under extremely difficult circumstances, which no doubt contributed to our marriage breakup.

Again and again I was told that getting a call would be difficult, if not impossible. "Have you looked elsewhere?" I was asked. My bishop, Herbert Chilstrom, shared my resume and a brief recommendation with the bishops of the church. I had direct personal contact with 12 bishops, explored possibilities with national and ecumenical agencies, and sent inquiries or application to 20 institutions of higher learning.

One bishop wrote that though my resume seemed promising, even impressive, he did not want his synod to become "a haven for divorced pastors." Other replies included: "You've got good credentials, but we have to face the reality of your divorce." "All the feedback about you and your work is positive, but the situation is very tight." "Nothing open at this time, have you tried . . .?" "Sorry, we have some openings, but nothing that would fit your profile." "Let's face it, your divorce is a definite factor."

Another bishop requested me to come to "look" at a possible congregation. I flew in to the city where the bishop's office was located for a brief interview. I was told that there was a congregation open and that he could arrange for a call to be extended. The terms, he indicated, were a salary of about half the average and a parsonage. He went on to say that he didn't want any "hanky panky" going on, and no "cleaning women" in the parsonage. I was sent to another city with his assistant to see the situation. Needless to say, I returned home without returning to the Bishop's office. I felt insulted, incensed! My low self-image at that time took a plunge. A mid-career assessment process had indicated I had strong skills for and interest in ministry. Was I to be denied from carrying out my call by the hierarchy of the church?

I did not feel I was expecting too much in terms of a salary and was willing to consider a variety of ministries, including single pastorates, staff and institutional positions. My frustration was evident when I said to one church executive, "God must be able to use me somewhere in the church!"

He pleaded, "Don't give up on us yet."

Yet I was becoming disillusioned with the institutional church as a viable means of justice in my case. Though I had been divorced for nearly two years, had made the adjustment to single life, and proven myself in ministry again and again, the divorce appeared to be the single factor that stood in the way of my receiving a viable call. One official indicated the difficulty of a divorced pastor getting called because of the system of recommending three names. He indicated that when there are two pastors with family and one alone, chances are slim.

"Now, if you had a wife, there would likely be no problem."
"Are you trying to tell me I should run out on the street and pick (up a wife)?" I asked.

"No," he replied, "But it sure would help."

I'm grateful that my bishop stuck by me. The congregation to which I received a call seemed to have a lot less difficulty with the fact that I was divorced and single than the bishops had.

Recovery Process

The recovery process was long. Gradually healing came, along with a sense of self-worth. There was an overwhelming sense of God's presence in my life in those times of struggle. My feelings in the heart of my pain seemed to be summed up in the verses of the Psalmist (109: 4-5): "I love them, but even while I am praying for them, they are trying to destroy me. They return evil for good and hatred for love."

I found strength, support, and help within the family of God. I made it a point to seek out a half-dozen or so good friends to "listen" and help me through the process of recovery. Some were professional pastoral care people; others were good friends and willing listeners. These persons demonstrated to me the true caring function of the fellowship of believers and I will remain indebted to them. I learned and experienced the importance of a caring Christian community.

I learned or relearned a number of other things about God and the church. I realized there can be a great difference between how I understand from scripture that God sees things and how the church views things. God's standards are different from the world's, even than bishops. God's grace is constantly available. God's validation of ministry is not dependent on worldly standards. God is greater than the church and individuals in it. Gradually, I began to see beyond the pain to the grace and hope that is possible in God's loving care, acceptance, and empowerment. I've learned that with God there is indeed justice.

Clowning around with kids 1978

Children's Recovery

Both Hiltje and Dane have had to suffer through a period as "third culture kids" with life within two cultures, trying to sort out and adjust to life around them. I am proud that they have done well in settling in the States. Both went through a period of trying to fit in the local scene, but have come to realize what a unique experience they had in childhood. Now they tell others openly of their life overseas.

Hiltje married an African American man who is a professor of American History at an Iowa University. She works as a hospital operator. They have two lovely daughters. One is in college and the other in high school.

Dane has been somewhat of a free spirit, trying out different options and, being the bolder of the two, in entering new ventures. Now in his late 40s, he has started a family and has two sons and a daughter. He resides in Denver and is an architect.

Life As A Single

The transition to single life was not easy. Dating, which seemed so natural earlier, was awkward. Having dated several women, I had some interesting encounters. But none of them (until Donna came along) really got me excited. I became comfortable being a single parent and forged relationships built on respect and common interests.

My ministry in mission awareness and interpretation was a natural for me. I built on what I had experienced over the years as I corresponded with congregations and visited them while on furlough. I was in demand as a speaker and wrote articles for synodical publications, including a booklet with a study guide on world mission. The first year I worked with the Minnesota Synod of the Lutheran Church in America. During this time I spoke at several retreats and events and visited congregations as requested. My goal was to organize (structures for mission) and plan for implementation.

Three things I was requested to do by Art Bauer and John Mangum, national Division of World Mission staff persons, are worth mentioning.

I was asked to serve as chaplain at a retreat for mission leaders in Chicago. I designed a worship format that was based on Indian worship which was innovative and appreciated.

I presented a paper on "Church Growth Principles and Lutheran Mission" to the board of the Division of World Mission for the Lutheran Church in America. In this paper I outlined some of the Donald McGavran / Peter Wagner (gurus of the church growth movement) principles and reflected on their usefulness in the Lutheran tradition. This was a new area of exploration for the board.

I was also requested to write a small book, later entitled "Cross Roads of World Mission," published by Parish Life Press in Philadelphia, for study by youth and adults.

The mission trip that I led to Southeast Asia included my mother and my IFYE mom, Esther Schmidt. There were 18 people and we were gone for nearly a month. I made all arrangements and handled all monies and tickets on the trip. Everyone seemed to enjoy the trip. There were several persons who had a 'conversion' experience of realizing that life is very different overseas and people there have much to teach us.

Based on that positive experience, the Division of World Mission explored the program the following year to include the upper midwest and central Canada areas. I did a lot of traveling visiting three Provinces of Canada and the states of Wisconsin, Illinois, Iowa, Nebraska, Michigan and the two Dakotas. Working together with synodical committees and staff persons, we developed structures and plans for mission awareness in each area. Then I proceeded to instruct leaders in mission.

I entered into this task with enthusiasm for I knew that the church was going through a period of decline in mission interest that needed to be revived. People at the grass roots level were excited, and I gave them an opportunity to voice their concerns. At the Synod Convention of the Red River Valley Synod, I was given a spontaneous standing ovation at the conclusion of my report.

During the summer of 1979 I led another group of church leaders to Asia that included an early visit to China, which had just opened up to the West.

My time with DWM was coming to a close. I knew that they could not extend the arrangement. DWM had gone out on a limb in creating my position, and I knew it had to come to an end. I corresponded with staff members of DWM and thanked them for their assistance and concern. They had been instrumental in getting me through a very difficult period and I was grateful.

But I was still without a call! Bishop Chilstrom made funds available to me for a couple of months while I pursued a call with vigor. Just when it seemed like I would have to take any employment to make ends meet, a congregation offered me a viable call.

11. PARISH LIFE IN THE STATES

Christ the Servant

In November of 1979 I began my first call to pastoral ministry in a congregation in the USA. The members of Christ the Servant Lutheran Church in Vadnais Heights, Minnesota, offered me a call. It was a small congregation of mostly blue-collar workers that had been on mission status (and thus dependent on support from synod) for 14 years. They were still in their first building unit in a growing suburb of St. Paul. When something needed to be done, there seemed to be a negative attitude of dependence on the part of leaders and members alike.

"Oh, we can't do that. Let's ask the synod for help, after all, we're only a small mission congregation." It took seven years of encouragement, development of a "we can do it" attitude, and a change of leadership before the pattern was broken.

There were lots of very good workers and persons of character who were dedicated to their church. But they did not have the confidence to get up and go on their own.

I enjoyed getting back into parish ministry again, visiting with people and calling in homes. I was asked to serve as chaplain to the city council, which gave me visibility and community connections. I was able to scrape together enough for a down payment on a condominium nearby in Little Canada. In nearly 20 years of service to the church I was not able to save anything, but did not expect to as a missionary.

Enter Donna

My private life had a big boost when one Donna Joy Ford showed up at my doorstep (introduced by a friend who had worked with her in Marshall, Minnesota). The circumstances of our getting together were unusual. Hiltje graduated from Armstrong High School in New Hope in June 1980. I had decided to take her with me on a trip to Europe as a graduation gift and as part of her education. I had gathered a group of friends and acquaintances that were interested in traveling to Europe on a trip that included the sites of the Reformation as well as the Oberammergau Passion Play. After a memorable trip through Germany, Switzerland, and Austria, Hiltje and I stayed on in Europe for a few days. We visited my IFYE families (it was great to see them all again and we spent time with Hiltje's namesake) and took a trip through Holland, Belgium, Luxemburg and France, visiting cathedrals and places of interest like Reims, Notre Dame, the Eiffel Tower, Versailles and the Louvre.

Before leaving the States, I had left the keys to my condo with a friend, Linda, and requested her to drop in and see that the place was OK and "looked lived in." Her friend, Donna, came to town for grad studies at the University and gave Linda a call, following up on a previous conversation to come and stay with her. In the meantime Linda had another friend staying at her place, but she had the keys for my place, which was empty and, after all, I had asked her to make sure it looked lived in. Hesitant, but reassured by Linda, Donna made the guest bedroom her place of residence during the short course she was taking. She was kind enough to write me a thank you note and offered to take me out to dinner the next time she was in town.

When we returned, I called my mother to check in, and she indicated that there was this girl at the condo when she and dad had dropped by to water the plants. Later, at our wedding dinner, we reenacted the scene when she came to the door and encountered my mother and father, teenage son Dane, and my ex-father-in-law. It was a hoot!

At any rate, Donna did come to town shortly after, called and invited me to dinner. I accepted even though I had already eaten. We had a brief but memorable courtship that included canoeing, a visit to the State Fair, golf, many meals out, visits to Marshall for me and the Twin Cities for her, and very focused conversations. This young woman who had obtained an education against all odds overwhelmed me. She came from a large family and a broken home, but had accomplished so much. She had skills in many areas, was a doctoral candidate, and was concluding her work as planner for the Educational Cooperative Service Unit (ECSU) for schools in Southwestern Minnesota. She had served as a teacher in the Native American program of North Dakota State University, making frequent visits to a reservation to teach Native Americans teacher education.

Attractive, vivacious, self-motivated and self-assured, Donna had made it in what up to that time had been a man's world: school administration. She was chosen as the only woman in her class in the prestigious Bush program and was in that program when I met her.

Wow, what a woman! She was a Lutheran, although inactive. I felt myself so fortunate to have met her. Our conversations focused on relationships, life goals, and faith. We were compatible and interested in similar things. She had traveled to Asia and Russia, liked international people, and was interested in exploring the world together. And it was important that she had an interest in my children and the ability to relate to them.

Donna was the answer to prayer and I thank God every day for her. She has been a true companion of faith. At first she was not as convinced as I that marriage was inevitable, but gradually the Lord showed her this was right and she has been a faithful, committed partner.

Our wedding, Dec. 26, 1980.
Valery Plummer, Donna, Duain and Dane

I digress, as I often do when I am speaking of Donna, for she is such a blessing. She was and has remained a breath of fresh air in my life. We were married on "Boxing Day," the day after Christmas, in 1980 at Christ the Servant Lutheran Church. We wanted the wedding to be a church- community event and it was. The church was already decorated (including wreaths that dad had made), the children's choir sang, and Pastors Norm Berg and Paul Sorlein officiated. It was a glorious day filled with friends and family, community spirit and good will. And for Donna and me, it was filled with love that has endured.

We had a delayed honeymoon in Hawaii. It was all that one could hope for as I introduced Donna to beautiful Hawaii. She fell in love with it we purchased a "time share" that was headquartered in Honolulu and have been back every two to three years since. I was deeply in love and desired to share all of life with Donna.

Donna continued her work in Marshall for a few months after we were married. She injured her back and was in great pain a good deal of the time. In spite of that, she continued taking courses toward her doctorate at the University of Minnesota. When she completed her course work and qualified to be a superintendent and principal, along with director of special ed, she had reached a milestone. Her skills were marketable and very much in demand and she was hired by school districts and the Minnesota Department of Education on a contract basis. As it turned out, this arrangement was much better for her as she had a steady and good income plus the flexibility of travel.

Donna and I continued to live in Canabury Square in a condo made from apartments. This was centrally located in Little Canada and was to be our home until departure to Florida. It was a comfortable, but not luxurious, home. Just north of St. Paul, it was convenient to our work and the various happenings in the Twin Cities, yet just a short distance from my old haunts in North St. Paul.

Visitors have always been welcome in our home. We have had people from around the globe visit us, dignitaries as well as ordinary folk. IFYEs, family, colleagues, travel partners, church leaders and missionaries – all are welcome, and we spend as much time as possible with them. Each one was a blessing. Many of these people have been from overseas, representing other cultures.

Back to Christ the Servant

We gathered for worship and other activities in the first unit built in the basic block construction of beginning churches. I eagerly entered into ministry, handling the various aspects of parish ministry with joy in spite of low pay and high demands. Christ the Servant was definitely a community church, the only church within the confines of the township at that time. We had lots of very basic blue-collar workers who took pride in their community. Sunday School, youth ministry, catechism, music for all ages, and adult education were offered.

One of the things I enjoyed most was taking youth on an annual boundary water canoe trip in northern Minnesota. We used an outfitter in Ely and launched our canoes from nearby, taking one of several round trips through the lakes and rivers for up to 10 days. We portaged several times, transporting canoes on our backs and tenting in a land that was pristine, without any motor traffic or buildings, full of the wonders of

God's great creation. And with rapids! I thoroughly enjoyed shooting rapids. My experience came from days at Camp Royaneh where I taught canoeing and a couple of trips that I had made with Atonement Lutheran Youth. It was good for character building and community.

I connected with Luther Seminary and students, as I had contact with the Global Mission Institute and had taught there. We were a contextual education center for the Seminary, meaning that candidates for ministry related to us, usually on a weekly basis, to get experience and become familiar with the demands of ministry. I took my responsibility seriously as site supervisor and tried to provide a well-rounded experience for students. I became attached to several of the students and participated as sponsor at their ordination. Eventually there were 17 such persons (four from Malaysia) that I felt extra close to in preparing them for ministry. Those at Christ the Servant were Jennifer Johnson, Nancy Amacher, Paul Huso, Paul Quist, Peter Ruggles and Stan Berntson (who was actually an intern when I left).

Meanwhile, with high visibility in the community (I rode in parades, organized the annual golf tournament, and was city chaplain) and a growing ministry, other people were attracted to the church. We continued to grow and attract newcomers, some of whom were white-collar folk. The Church Council was made up increasingly of new people. I saw this as a hopeful sign, but it posed a threat to the old guard.

As we expanded the work at Christ the Servant, brought in some new blood, and looked at possibilities for the future development of the church, it was clear that we needed a new building. A capital fund drive brought pledges that fell short of estimated costs. Lacking the funding to go the traditional route, we decided to build the church ourselves using the skills and willingness of members and friends. We had quite a few individuals with building skills and lots of willing painters and gophers. An architect was hired and came up with a plan that was accepted. Duane Heacock was hired as our construction manager. Unfortunately, he dropped his medical insurance for a brief period and was diagnosed with cancer after the building was completed. We had special fund-raising events for him.

He served the church well, putting in many hours and guiding the various groups that did the various projects.

Volunteers provided meals for workers during the evening hours. For several months there was a flurry of activity and a "we can do it" attitude. The esprit de corps was high as we went through the building program. Since I did not have any skills in building, I continued with my regular ministry. Donna, knowing that the building program was important to the church and a step that would lead to another call, was willing to serve as co-chair of the building committee with the proviso that the other co-chair would handle all monies.

When the building was completed, the congregation could finally say, "We did it" with pride and a promising future. Dedication of our new facility occurred in the fall of 1986. It was time for me to move on and though members at Christ the Servant were sorry to see me go, I looked for new challenges.

Our Redeemer Lutheran Church

The call to ORLC came at the end of 1986. It was not a healthy situation or congregation. It had been through a traumatic series of events that left it hurting, searching for direction. They had been through a period of inappropriate sexual involvement on the part of pastors and an intern. If I was going to be effective as their Pastor, I needed to build trust. This took a long time.

The congregation had 1,600 people on the rolls. It was clear that with about 200 worshiping, my work was cut out for me. I cleaned the rolls down to about 1,200 and began calling at homes. I was the sole Pastor for most of years I was there. In retrospect this was a mistake, but we were hurting financially and it took years to turn that around. I should have said, "Either I get help, or I'm out of here." I entered into ministry enthusiastically, taking on all aspects of ministry. While I planned to be solo through the first year, it dragged on much too long. I lost my edge and could not see the forest for the trees. I was too busy and exhausted to keep my focus on the overall mission and provide the kind of creative thinking and leadership that was necessary. Dianne Biever served as my secretary for the first few years at ORLC and friend, Lorna Peck, later.

Not that it started out that way. I thoroughly enjoyed ministry for several years. I celebrated my 30th anniversary of ordination two and a half years into my work there. It was a memorable, celebrative event. Donna worked on it behind the scenes and orchestrated the whole event. It was a most memorable occasion and lots of fun as several persons from my past were there and several spoke. My mother spoke of my early life and State 4-H Leader Leonard Harkness also spoke. Ramsey County 4-H leaders were there as well as Esther Schmidt, my IFYE Mom. Delano Mottaz and Herb Ketchem represented my high school class, and Norm Berg my seminary years. Emery Barrette told of Hamline Golf Team days. To my surprise the bishop appeared, as did members of Christ the Servant Church. The whole senior choir sang. Pastor Rees honored me by speaking. Pastor Jenny Johnson represented seminary students I had nurtured in ministry.

The program went on for a long time as persons got into telling stories about me, most of which were true. My old music teacher, choir and band director, Palmer Rauk, was there with his wife Margaret (my old piano teacher) and sang a tune that told life stories. They were too kind and complementary. I was overwhelmed and humbled. To top off the evening, Dane spoke and presented me with a humorous golfing caricature that he drew. Then he and Hiltje, on behalf of the whole family, presented me with a bronze sculpture by Paul Granlund, famous Minnesota artist from Gustavus Adolphus College and my former teacher of ceramics. When I got up to speak I felt surrounded by a great cloud of witnesses down through the years which had played a major role in who I had become. I was deeply grateful. Shirley Sorenson wrote a poem summarizing the event.

After, reflecting on the events of that evening, I wrote:

In a life time
> Few have been blessed as I
> With people and events extraordinary
> With opportunities for serving
> With caring family and friends

With a Lord who forgives and challenges
> sends to the far corners of the globe
> calls to minister among those in need
> and provides the Spirit to give vision.

In a life time
> There are less than a handful of happenings
> that are so overwhelming in scope
> and touch the heart so deeply

As to be cherished and remembered
> Above all others.

Such a time for me was May 18, 1990.

There were some true saints at Our Redeemer who stuck with it through thick and thin. Among them were Dennis and Jan Peterson, Dan and Shirley Sorenson, Elmo and June Mattox, Carol and Doug Watnemo, Tom and Helen Wallace, Mary and Randy Luhrs, the Heimerdingers and the Kozas. There was a core group of strong, qualified, lay leaders without whom a congregation cannot move forward. "The Growing Place" was our theme for several years as we did some things to spruce up the facilities and organize for growth. I had done my contextual education work while a seminary student at Our Redeemer when it was a mission congregation. It was a friendly place where I gained experience as a future pastor.

Key to getting persons back to church was creating an atmosphere of acceptance. There were a lot of hurting people who needed to be heard and healed. Our music program was a real blessing. With Dick Williams (paid) and Ned Potter (unpaid) at the keyboards and Marshal Johnson as senior choir director, the quality of music was high. Indeed it was of a quality that one would expect from a church much larger than our own. Gradually we began to increase attendance, to over 300, which was good considering the changing neighborhood and general climate of the congregation.

We had a full-blown youth and catechetical program, an active Sunday School, senior citizens group, adult Bible studies, men's and women's groups. In addition, there was a group of shut-ins who expected monthly calls. In addition, there were tons of meetings that kept me at the church -- sometimes for several days running. I would go home, collapse for a few hours, and return. People's expectations were higher than one person could fulfill. When I approached the mutual ministry committee about taking a sabbatical, the concept appeared to be foreign and unacceptable.

We had some excellent youth retreats at St. Mark's, my old home church. At both Christ the Servant and Our Redeemer, Lutheran Youth Encounter International Teams provided an annual event. I served on the national board of Youth Encounter for a number of years.

One of the enjoyable parts of ministry was nurturing seminary students through parish ministry. I would be especially close to those who responded to my personal history and style of discussion -- teaching and obtaining responses from them. Mike Rozumalski came from being in a Roman Catholic Order. Later his wife, Linda, largely responsible to getting Mike on track, would complete her seminary training and be ordained. Jeff Teeples came with a solid spirituality. John Weisenberger had been with us in Africa when he made the decision to go to seminary. Clint Pickett came through the military and served briefly in a parish before going back into a military career. Steve Mahan and Tom Anderson were second career people with lots of experience in life. Each one had unique contributions to make. I have tried to keep in contact with them since then. Two of my ordinands have passed away. Michael Maran met with a tragic fatal accident in Malaysia just after reporting for a new parish. Steve Mahan had a rare disease that struck him down at the height of his ministry. These students distinguished themselves and served well.

One of the things I recall fondly was decorating the church during Advent each year. We would have a party for all ages and make decorations for home and church. I remember teaching kids and adults how to make wreaths, yule logs, and Chrismons. I made a design for the sanctuary each year, utilizing trees from the pine forest, some decorated, but most of them natural to decorate the chancel and extend through the church. Poinsettia plants were placed about to give color. It was a glorious sight, giving a special effect and meaning to the season celebrating the birth of Christ. The smell of pine was in the air and the story of the Word becoming flesh took on new meaning .

12. KEEPING MISSION INTEREST

A Vision That Would Not Die:
The Global Mission Institute
At Luther Seminary

There have been times in my life when I have felt a conviction to step out and act, moved by a higher power to tackle the powers that be to bring about change. There are even fewer times when it was necessary to start something from scratch that made a difference in an institution's direction and made a profound effect, not only on the institution, but also a large community related to it. It was truly the Lord's leading as we ventured out to address a concern we shared. In working with others who shared my passion for mission, the vision to establish the Global Mission Institute at Luther Seminary unfolded over a number of years.

When I began relating to congregations in the States I heard concern that the church had lost its focus on mission. Significant areas that had traditionally been hotbeds for mission were voicing concern. The cry came to us: "What has happened to global mission in the church?" Some of this was addressing the reality of the changes in the missionary enterprise. It was carried out in different ways. But the concern of a significant number of persons of the place of global mission could not be ignored.

Three of us former missionaries were in the Minnesota Synod of the Lutheran Church in America (LCA). Bob Engwall and Dwight Johnson had come out of the Augustana Synod, a church that had a tradition of strong mission support. Each of us was involved in lifting up global mission throughout the Synod, speaking at various functions, attending meetings and writing. There was reason for concern. Our discussion focused on the need for a renewed focus on mission at our seminary. If the church was going to have a renewed interest in mission, pastors would play a key role and the theological training they received would need to be focused on mission.

We decided to take action from the congregations of the church, from the grassroots. These concerns were brought before the two LCA Synods (Minnesota and Red River Valley) who directly supported Northwestern Seminary. In June 1977 identical resolutions were proposed and overwhelmingly approved at both synod conventions to call congregations and members to take up this cause and work with the seminary in addressing global mission awareness and education. An ad hoc committee was established a year later with participants from the two synods.

The three of us (Johnson, Engwall, and me) were joined by persons from the Red River Valley Synod. Lloyd Zaudkte was a valuable resource. The Minnesota Synod included Betty Anderson and Lorna Peck. Paul Martinson joined us from the faculty and Ron Lundeen from the development staff.

We had a vision of a seminary that would be for Lutherans what Fuller had become for Protestantism. Mission would take a place on the center stage of theological education. The mission enterprise of the church might view Luther Seminary as a leader, with advanced degrees offered by qualified missiologists, where serious research would take place and meaningful research published.

Progress was slow, but God would not let the vision die. We gathered momentum in the early 80s raising funds from the grassroots; individuals, congregations, and mission groups from the two synods were assisted by grants from Gloria Dei Lutheran Church in St. Paul. We desired to have an identity with local congregations and a program that included them. The GMI Task Force focused on mission education both within the seminary and to the congregations and individuals of the church. International student support, library resources, and assistance in faculty teaching overseas assisted the seminary directly, while the establishment of the "Cross Change" program, an Annual Lutheran Mission Conference, and visits to congregations strengthened ties at the grassroots level.

The "Cross Change" programs provided an overseas mission seminar for church members interested in deepening ties overseas. There were two: one to East Africa and one to India and Nepal that Donna and I had the privilege of leading in 1987.

The Annual Lutheran Mission Conference was popular and brought together resources and speakers on mission in a day-long focus that lifted up global mission. Over 500 from congregations in the upper Midwest, including some from Missouri Synod, participated. It was a marvelous tool of mission awareness for congregations and individuals until its demise after nearly 20 years of existence. GMI gave leadership and support to this effort in cooperation with the Association of Lutheran Mission Committees.

The initial goal was to establish an endowed chair of missiology at Luther Northwestern Seminary (the two schools were in the process of merging, later to be known as Luther Seminary). This fledging start was not immediately helpful to the seminary. It was clear, however, that there were individuals and congregations concerned about the future of mission education at the Seminary and in the church.

With the full merger of the two seminaries and the endowment of a chair of mission by the American Lutheran Church, Duane Olson came to fill that position and was appointed by President Svendsbye as the first director of the newly established Global Mission Institute. I was chosen as chair of the newly formed executive council, a position I served until 1994.

There was activity within the life of the seminary that was related to mission and globalization. There were a variety of electives, a newly started Cross-Cultural Program, visits by international leaders, lectures by visiting professors. GMI incorporated a number of these activities under its umbrella.

Rev. Dr. David Preus, former bishop and head of the American Lutheran Church, became the part-time director of GMI, and Charlotte Gronseth became associate director. Dr. Preus provided visibility and Gronseth handled the bulk of the work.

In spite of this growing responsibility there were problems in identifying the focus of GMI. This was due in part to the fact that GMI had its feet in two places. One was rooted in the grass roots whence it came and the other in the seminary itself. In a sense it was a "sodality" attempting to operate within a "modality" of the church.

The GMI continued to influence the seminary to focus on mission. The seminary continued to expand its program overseas. Paul Martinson led a series of seminars to China. Dr. Lee Snook in Zimbabwe had started a program called "Global Vision Africa." Contact with overseas churches was escalating. The Andrew Burgess Lectureship was started in 1991. Other programs were initiated among students and faculty. Changes in the curriculum indicated a change in the direction of the seminary.

Dr. David l. Tiede, new president of Luther Seminary wrote a memorandum to the GMI Executive Committee in April 1992. "We are at a very critical and creative moment in the history of the Global Mission Institute and its mission at Luther Northwestern Theological Seminary. The conversations that we have held since January of this year have clarified and strengthened the role of the Global Mission Institute and established an agenda for work that will extend through the next several years. We are now facing a time of significant transition..."

Tiede went on a trip through Southeast and East Asia with a small group of people that included me. In a conversation that took place between the two of us 35,000 feet over the China Sea, we spoke of the future of GMI and its role in the seminary. It was clear that if GMI were to be a player in the transformation of the seminary, it would have to become integrated into the life of the school.

When we returned, a new era of cooperation began as the board of GMI was reorganized integral to Luther Seminary. Dr. Henry French, academic dean, was instrumental in facilitating the integration process. Other faculty members (Steve Charleston, Terry Fretheim, Dan Simmundson, Mark Thomson, Rod Maeker, Wendel Frerichs, and Peri Rosolondraibe) lent their weight to the discussion.

Dr. Preus concluded his service in mid 1994. I had gone on disability in 1993 and moved to Florida. I was appointed to take an interim part-time position as interim director of GMI and served until October of 1996. I was unsalaried. Gronseth continued her service. In 1995 an operational plan helped to clarify the place of GMI in the life of the seminary and its objective; "To educate and equip leaders for Christian communities to make disciples of all nations and to serve in God's world."

The table had been set for the next era of GMI at Luther Seminary. Tiede wrote in 1996 that "Luther Seminary is now able to name and claim the GMI's strategic value." The Islamic Studies Program under the leadership of Dr. Roland Miller, had already started. Miller, with experience in India as a missionary and in Canada as a teacher and administrator, was a strong advocate for mission. "The Congress on the World Mission of the Church: St. Paul '98" was his vision. It brought together mission thinkers and practitioners from around the globe to a distinctly Lutheran setting. It is unfortunate that the impact of this gathering was somewhat muted and did not receive the recognition it deserved in the Lutheran community. This was partly due to the selection process and to follow up. However, it turned the church's attention to realize that Luther Seminary had something important to say.

Dr. Paul Martinson edited a volume of papers presented (entitled "Mission at the Dawn of the 21st Century; a Vision for the Churches").

In addition to the general papers, there were eleven areas of focus. Six were geographical: Africa, China, Former Soviet Union (The "Eastern Block"), India, Latin America and North America. Five were topical: Theology, Service, Structures, Education and Information Technology. I was privileged to be asked to write the "status" paper on structures for mission, and be a participant in the conference. It was an affirming experience, though I found myself somewhat removed from the center of mission thought, since I was living in Florida.

When I left in October 1996, Craig Moran was appointed as faculty director of GMI. Since then, there has been a gradual and purposeful move in focusing Luther Seminary on mission. Rather than courses on mission topics, the whole curriculum and life at the school is missional. The very character and thrust of Luther is on mission. This, of course, is the fulfillment of the vision we had when we formed the GMI, but it is much better defined and articulated. Current leadership, with Richard Bliese as president, has the challenge now of bringing other theological schools and the church back to an evangelical understanding of scripture and an emphasis that holds up biblical preaching and teaching in the development of leaders of mission.

Nijhar Minz

One of the great joys of ministry at the seminary has been the opportunity to get to know a number of the international students. None has been dearer to me than Nijhar Minz. She came to Luther Seminary in 1994 with a strong desire to be trained in America and bring her distinct contributions to the church here. She is a vivacious, articulate women who is not afraid to witness verbally to her faith. She had received her basic theological education in India, then traveled to the States on a one way ticket. Exploring various options for study in America, she settled on Luther Seminary. But she was unsupported. She came to me at GMI one August day with a smile and a note from her father, Nirmal Minz, and bishop of the Northwest Gossner Lutheran Church in India that the "Cross-Change" group of 1987 had visited in the Ranchi area.

The note was a greeting from her father and a request that I do whatever I could to provide contacts for Nijhar among congregations here. I'm sure he knew and had the faith that once people from congregations heard Nijhar, support for her education would come forth. Indeed it did! Her spirit and personality attracted people to her. In time she served as a part-time staff member of GMI. When I was on campus I often would visit with her. We became close friends in Christ. We shared a passion for mission. We regularly ate meals together.

As the years passed, she (who had been born in USA and thus an American citizen) returned to India, got ordained, and married. Her pull to Luther Seminary was so strong that she returned with her husband. He worked on his PhD in theology and she has yet to complete her doctorate at the University of Minnesota. Her parents also came to the States on a sabbatical before retirement. In time she had children, four in fact. Three of them were born in the States. Maani, Urbas, and Puna came in quick succession. It was amazing how they could manage a large family, take studies seriously, work part time, and still manage to have significant contact with congregations.

After 10 years in the States, Nijhar returned to India with her family in 2005, having her final child, Jumpha, in India. She and her husband, Neeraj, had a vision for a theological training center that would serve their people. They shared the vision with Donna and me and together we worked at enlisting congregations who were willing to support their vision. Besides our local congregation, Hope Lutheran Church in The Villages, Florida and neighboring St. John Lutheran Church, a group of congregations in the upper Midwest have provided funding. The story of my personal involvement in this project will be told later.

Neeraj and Nijhar Minz-Ekka and their family have made several visits to us in Florida and we have been to Ranchi, India, twice since then in 2004 and 2007.

Canoeing

To be outside taking advantage of God's great creation during summers in the upper Midwest is one of the many delights. Life becomes a playground with over 10,000 natural lakes in Minnesota alone. Many make it a point to escape to their cabins "at the lake" and enjoy the water. For those who seek adventure, camping and travel by canoe is an exciting opportunity.

After returning to the States, I turned to canoeing. It has provided the opportunity to enjoy God's great creation in its natural setting, get away from the demands of ministry, get good exercise and have time with my son. We have taken trips down the Nemakagen, Kettle, Cannon, St. Croix (Upper and Lower), and Minnesota Rivers. Shooting the rapids was an activity that was both challenging and liberating. It has been exhilarating to weave our way down rapids up to number three (out of four) on the rating scale, with water splashing in our faces.

But seeing God's great creation has been the greatest benefit. Once Dane and I were paddling down the Kettle River early in the morning. It was one of those magical moments when the water was high and there was mist in the air. As we came around a bend in the river, we startled a doe and her fawn who were out, knee deep in the water, drinking. The doe ran for the shore as she spotted us, but the poor fawn froze in her tracks in the water. We passed by so close that we could reach out and touch the fawn. The doe watched anxiously from the shore.

Minnesota has a vast area along the Canadian border, known as the boundary canoe area, that is a haven for canoeists. The wilderness stretches for hundreds of miles and is without buildings and motors of any sort. It is great place to take a group of youth and learn to work together. I took a group of young people up to the boundary water area for several days each year. We had an outfitter near Ely, Minnesota, set us on a journey that took us to the Canadian border and beyond and then back down to a designated place some seven to ten days later. We took a chain of lakes in each direction, guided by a map, planning portages and camping sites along the way. We carried canoes on our shoulders, food, and camping equipment in backpacks. There is great community building as you face together the many tasks of a canoe trip in the wilderness. Finding your way through the mirage of lakes to the next portage, seeing wild life along the way (moose were prevalent), drinking pure water from the lake, washing dishes in the lake and finding time for fishing – these were part of the challenges and joys of canoeing.

Food of any kind had to be hung up between trees for the night or the bears would smell even candy bars and somehow rip open backpacks. There were numerous encounters with more than one bear. Once it snowed and we were pressed to keep warm and dry when it rained. But these were offset by the sheer delight of being out in such a beautiful, awesome world.

The Celebration of Culture

While we were located in the Twin Cities, we tried to take advantage of the wide variety of cultural events that were offered. It was like a great sea of opportunity to be explored, hindered only by our pocketbook, our worldly commitments, and mind limitations. The Twin Cities area offers a plethora of events in a wide variety of expression supported by a generous and beneficiate group of companies. We had season tickets to the symphony and the Guthrie Theatre. We took advantage of rush lines and discounts. There were many live theatres, from experimental to classical. One of my most memorable evenings was a concert of Tschaikovsky's Piano Concerto #1 by van Cliburn, who had just returned from Russia where he had won the Tschaikovsky competition. It was at Northrup Auditorium at the University of Minnesota and I went with Esther Schmidt. The performance was electrified and the crowd mesmerized. There were numerous encores.

Then there were a number of opportunities to attend programs that featured other cultures, like India or China. The "Festival of Nations" is a celebration of diversity.

With the colleges nearby, especially Lutheran, there were sacred concerts that were of high quality. I still would like to travel to the Upper Midwest during early Advent and be in on concerts by the music departments of Gustavus Adolpus, Concordia, St. Olaf, Luther, and Augsburg Colleges. It would be a touch of heaven. The concerts on national public TV are good, but one does not get the spirit of the students and the worshipful attitude that is conveyed in the original settings.

There is a variety of art museums: the Institute of Art, the Walker, and the new Russian Art Museum are just the cream of the crop. Attending events at these institutions leaves one with a desire to celebrate the arts and a God who provides so much creativity to flourish. The special exhibitions they provide are outstanding.

Of course we just barely tapped the opportunity that was there. We had full, busy lives. The true blessing of these cultural events was not fully realized by us until we moved away. We give thanks that they were available and we could take advantage of some of them. The influence of such a wealth of artistic opportunity is colossal, touching teaching and amateur groups and individuals alike. I am grateful that I had this available. But I am even more grateful for the opportunities I had to be exposed to the wide variety of cultures around the globe. God has richly blessed me with countless encounters with people of unique cultures in Asia, Africa, and Latin America, as well as Europe and America.

Travel With a Difference

It was a joy to facilitate this ministry. We considered this an extension of our ministry because lives were changed. The people who traveled with us most were Gordy and Betty Lundberg (who hold the record of eight or nine times), Bob and Marianne Sanders, Roger and Carole Longenecker, Helen Hammersten, Jack and Judy Pirkl, Charles and Marilyn Jacobson, and the Weisenburgers (Bob, Bonnie and John). They brought an attitude each day that this was a day to be embraced and could hardly wait to get started on the journey. With them along, it was hard not to have a fun time! They had confidence and trust in Donna and me to make the right decisions.

We faced some tough decisions. One was to stay for the night in East Berlin or West Berlin during the days of the DDR (Deutsche Democratic Republic). When possible, we let the group decide.

On another occasion, Palestinians were launching missiles, attacking the Israeli settlement in Golan Heights, causing some damage. The guide asked me what we should do. I said that my understanding from reading the news was that these attacks were held each morning and that when the Israeli reconnaissance appeared, the missile launchers were hidden and deactivated. "That is correct," she stated, "but we have no guarantee." I decided we should go, knowing that we could turn back if necessary. The day went well, although some on the bus saw the damage en route.

On more than one occasion we were cornered in crowded conditions. We would put the strongest individuals on the sides interlock arms, and then I would lead a wedge through the crowd, thus avoiding pickpockets and others who took advantage of tourists. There were, of course, a variety of illnesses and accidents, but none so serious that we had to send someone home.

It was a joy to take visitors on a mission trip through Southeast Asia. As I directed the bus, our young guide commented: "You know Malaysia better than I." At the end of a trip through Asia I took a group for a few days into China just after it had opened again in 1979. With all the images that the Chinese had of Americans I cautioned our group to err on the side of being gracious rather than confrontive. Unfortunately the China travel agency placed another smaller group with us and made me the leader.

On our final night in China there was a "Friendship Dinner" in which Chinese put their best foot forward in trying to impress us. Our group sang which was appreciated by our hosts. When we were about to leave our Chinese hosts came to us and said one of the cloisonné trays was missing. I knew it was not one of our group members but could not speak for the other group. Our solution was to go back to the bus and share the problem with passengers, then we turned out the bus lights and had passengers file out and I told them that I expected the tray to be on the front seat when the lights were turned on. It was and we returned the tray, but the damage had been done. In overseas travel it is so important to be culturally sensitive.

When we left for India in July 1986 we were faced with a tough decision. Dad's Parkinson's was advanced, so I said my goodbyes and left for the trip with the understanding that Donna would take over leadership of the group of 23 if I had to return. We had just arrived in India when news came of Dad's passing. I did what I could to make arrangements for the group and left on a flight to the States. I arrived in time for the visitation, and attending the funeral the next day. After a day with my Mom I flew back to join the group in India. By now they had moved on to Hyderabad and my name had been removed from the group, so there were difficulties, but I was able to catch up with the group and get some rest, but it was not until days later that I was able to take over leadership. In less than a week's time I had flown over 30,000 miles!

During 1986 some of the group visited Ranchi and were privileged to associate with Bishop Nirmal Minz of the Northwest Gossner Lutheran Church. This was a church and a people that we would become so involved with later.

Donna and I facilitated a group, primarily of Episcopalians with Father Steve Raulerson, to the Holy Land in 1996. We had a Palestinian Christian guide, who understandably since his job security was tied into tolerance of the state, was reluctant to share his feelings about the Israelis treatment of Palestinians. Then well into the experience our group was scheduled to spend the day in Jerusalem, including the Wailing Wall and the temple mount (site of Solomon's Temple and sacred to Christian, Jews, and Muslims).

We presented ourselves at the Dung Gate close to the temple mount. Going to the security gate we were stopped by the guards. I asked our guide what was the problem. He was being refused entry and his papers were questioned. We pleaded with the young guards to no avail and they refused entry of our guide. Waiving our group by to go to the Wailing Wall, I questioned the guards further. It was clear that for some reason they were keeping our Palestinian guard from entering. Getting nowhere with the gate guards, I requested to see their supervisor. When he came, he could not tell me specifically what was wrong with the papers of our guide. I told him that his credentials had not been questioned at any of the other places we went. He was leading this group of Americans and was needed. Unless he wanted a complaint from the group he should let our guide in. The guide could not plead his own cause, so it was necessary for me, as leader, to be his advocate. Finally, 10 minutes before the gate to the temple mount closed, they allowed him in. Never before had our guide experienced a group leader who advocated for him. He was grateful which was evident in his continuing leadership. Later we met with leaders of the Lutheran Church in Palestine and learned more of the problems faced by these oppressed people. When I returned to the States, I found out the real reason why our guide had been stopped that day. It seems an Israeli guide had been stopped in Bethlehem and a tit for tat operation was put into operation.

It is difficult to understand the problems faced in the Holy Land. Americans do not get an accurate picture from the media. The voice of the Palestinians need to be heard. Both sides need to repent and start anew, but it is difficult with such a long history of conflict.

With Donna in New Zealand 1991

On the Move...with the Master

Overseas Trips led by Duain and
(after 1980) with Donna

YEAR

1978	Hong Kong, Singapore, Malaysia, Sumatra (Indonesia); and Philippines – Minnesota Synod sponsored – Duain
1979	Malaysia, Singapore, Thailand, Hong Kong, and China Synod sponsored – Duain
1980	Europe (Eastern and Western Germany, Austria, and Switzerland)
1983	Europe (Eastern and Western Germany, Denmark and Norway) (With Norm Berg)
1984	Jordan, Holy Land and Europe (Oberammergau)
1985	Malaysia, Singapore, Thailand, Hong Kong, and China.
1986	India and Nepal
1988	Tanzania and Kenya
1989-90	Australia, New Zealand, and Fiji
1992	Israel and Rome
1992	Singapore, Malaysia, Hong Kong, China, and Japan -- Seminaries Scotland
1995	Journeys of Paul (Greece & Turkey)(With Carl Fisher)
1996	Sweden, Finland & St. Petersburg (Russia)
1996	Israel
1997	Alaska

Our trip to East Africa in 1988 offered us a chance to see wild life and experience life in the church at the same time. For the game parks we were in the hands of missionary kids who had stayed on in Tanzania after their parents retired. The time in the church was divided with visits to local churches mixed in with the national Lutheran church. We were impressed and inspired by the people as they worshipped for hours and women piercing the air with a unique glottal trill whenever they were pleased, as they were when our small group of visitors formed a choir and sang for them. These people were amazingly happy and content with what would be for us, little.

In 1999 we took a Panama Canal cruise with visits to several of the Caribbean Islands. In 2002 and 2003 we cruised in the Southern and Western Caribbean. I was chaplain on a Western Caribbean Cruise over Christmas 2005.

Earlier I reported that I visited Europe with daughter Hiltje in 1980. In addition, Donna and I have taken the several trips abroad. 1981 we honeymooned in Hawaii and went back in 1982, but managed in a trip to Acapulco in between. In 1983 we visited Lorraine Valley and Nice in France and in 1984 we added a brief stop in Holland at the end of our Oberammergau trip. The next five years we took weeklong respites in Acapulco in the winter. We were in Hawaii again in 1990, 1993, 1996,1998, 2001 2004 and 2007. We visited Acapulco again in 1991 and did not visit again until 1999. On trips through Europe, a stop in Holland was important to renew relationships, visit family, and rest.

In March of 2000 I took a trip to Holland and Germany to visit family and then again 2006. In the summer of 2003, Donna and I, accompanied by brother Tijte, took a lovely trip (in conjunction with the World IFYE Conference) through the Netherlands, Denmark, Sweden, and Germany combined with a trip to the U.K. to visit friends. We had a wonderful time with excellent companions on a trip through Italy after our India trip. I also visited Guyana and Suriname twice in conjunction with my position on the Florida-Bahamas Global Mission Committee.

The questions are often put to us: "Why do you travel so much and why do you go to the countries you do." We enjoy travel, although it has become more demanding as of late (a combination of our health and the restrictions placed on travel within the industry). I enjoy the challenge of getting to know new people and places, of becoming acculturated to new surroundings. The opportunity for personal growth is unique. Meeting new friends is a privilege. Getting to observe the Body of Christ and the manner in which she has adapted is fascinating. I never cease to be amazed on the way in which fellow Christians around the globe receive us. It is truly a blessing.

When Donna and I got married, one of the things we agreed upon was travel, but not just for getting somewhere, but also for exploring peoples and cultures. Little did we know that we would travel as much as we have. It was a joy to do it together, for we complimented one another and shared the load. I would generally work out the itinerary, do the correspondence with overseas leaders, and lead the group. Donna would bring up the rear of the group, keep charge of the money, deal with complaints, and offer advice on how the group is doing. And when required, as was the case when I had to return to the States because of my Father's death, she was willing and able to lead. The group experiences we offered almost always included the component of contact and interaction with local people, whether it be Swedes on midsummer's eve, Palestinians who were without voice and home, or Tribal peoples in Africa proud of their heritage and church.

Those who traveled more than once with us said that the reason they kept coming back was that we offered them a chance to mingle with local people, to grow in understanding and faith. There were some truly life-changing experiences. Many had their eyes (and minds) opened to a new worldview. They viewed and understood things from a new perspective. God uses such experiences to renew us and allow us to see a larger world than what we had previously known. We begin to see through the eyes and cultures of others. And through others our faith is challenged and matures.

13. RETIREMENT

The Fall

After returning from Scotland in 1992 and the emotional high of that memorable journey with Emery, I settled back into the routine of parish ministry at Our Redeemer. On the morning of August 14, I got up to shower and go to work. Donna went to the condo pool for a swim. When she returned, she found me standing by the sink asking the question "Had I shaved?" over and over. I had shaved but had no memory of doing so. I was disoriented and confused. She then noticed that I had bruises on my back and arms and a bump on my head. Apparently I had blacked out and fallen.

Donna ended up taking me to the doctor who admitted me into the hospital for tests. They did not find anything. I had been experiencing dizzy spells for several months, including one at Synod Convention. After the fall these spells increased and I was uneasy on my feet and could not drive for a few weeks. I went back to work, managed to get along with help in driving and gradually my condition seemed to be improving. Medically I was on a schedule of numerous tests, but none of them showed anything.

At work I finally received some help. Steve Mahan graduated from seminary and joined the staff as associate pastor. Steve had been interested in returning to Texas where he had been a fireman. When a call did not come, it seemed like God had a call for him right where he was at Our Redeemer. Since he had been a member, the congregation knew him well and was open to extending a call. Although I had help, there was also the added pressure of keeping the ship going when I was not well. I managed to make it through the Christmas season and into January doing little else than work.

The Collapse

On the morning of January 14, 1993, I had an early morning appointment with the newspaper. During the meeting I had been experiencing some back pain. Returning to the office at church, I collapsed on the floor. I was in excruciating pain but managed to get up and asked Steve to take me to Donna's chiropractor nearby. He worked on me but did not completely get rid of my back spasms. I managed to drive home to rest, but I never experienced the severe pain I knew during that time. I called Donna and was hyperventilating on the phone. For three days I went back to the chiropractor, but when he realized that there was something more than he could address, he suggested I go for tests, which I did. So I entered another barrage of tests. In the meantime I carried on work as best I could.

We felt that it would be good to get away from the demands and winter weather. It had been our practice for several years to go to Acapulco for a break. When my tests did not seem to turn up anything, Donna flew down to Acapulco and I was to join her later in the week. I had one more test, an abdominal CT scan on February 16. I knew something was up when they also proceeded to scan the upper and lower portions of my abdomen.

The doctor met with me immediately and told me that I faced a major problem that would require surgery within the next 24 hours. I had a dissecting aortic aneurysm, which in many cases is fatal. That afternoon I called Donna and she returned to be with me. The next day I met with surgeons. They conferred and said that they decided they would not operate as the tear in my aorta ran from the left subclavin artery to the right iliac, nearly two feet in length. It would take three surgeries with a 25 per cent morality rate with each surgery. I had survived for a month and they recommended I go to the Mayo Clinic for treatment which I did. I went on medical leave.

I got appointments with doctors in Rochester, Minnesota. Thus began a relationship that would last the rest of my life. I was put on a medication that kept me sedated a great deal of the time, then the dosage was cut in half and cut again so I could function. I went to the swimming pool each day to exercise in a relatively weightless situation. I developed a form of meditative Tai Chi that was helpful.

But I succumbed to depression. Confined to our condo much of the time, the winter months left me with a sense of hopelessness. I did not lose my faith in God and kept contact with people, keeping up a schedule of meetings like GMI and Cassette Group, but it was difficult to see beyond my current condition. I applied for disability with the ELCA Board of Pensions and within a week's time it was granted. When we left for a vacation in Florida the end of March, I called the president of the church and told him I had decided to resign as senior pastor of Our Redeemer Lutheran Church. It was difficult to do this as we had entered a time when I felt we were ready to do some innovative things, but that was not to be the case with my leading the flock.

Florida

When we arrived in Florida, the reality of my resignation and the future was before us. Donna and I had attended a workshop on retirement when I reached the age of 50. At that time we had agreed that we wanted to retire in a warm climate. We began exploring different options. We ruled out California, then Arizona, and Arkansas. When we visited North Carolina, we were impressed with friends and golfing properties but did not find a place that offered activities and education that we felt were important. We liked the fact that the flora and fauna were beautiful, but the climate was a bit too cold for Donna. So when we came to Florida, we were looking for the ideal spot.

We explored the Ft. Myers area where Donna's sister lived, but found it too hot and too expensive. We had seen an advertisement for an offer to visit The Villages located between Leesburg and Ocala in Central Florida. We could stay for a few days in a house and get our money back to enjoy golf or taste some of the amenities offered. We called and got a place during the first days of April. We found it to be delightful with housing in our price range and a growing activity program. We liked the basic philosophy that all were welcome and paid the same amenity fee. The cost of living seemed to be manageable and there were many lakes and lots of trees. We looked at possible sites while there, but made no decision.

Returning to Minnesota, we were convinced that The Villages was the place for us. So we called and booked a place and house (which could be built in short order). It would be close to a town square and on the second of several golf courses. We decided that we did not want to face the golf course and chose one of the less expensive lots across the street. The developers had the policy that if you came down to order the house and made decisions about the plan, they gave you VIP treatment including a stretch limo at the airport. My mother came with us along with our daughter, Hiltje. They enjoyed the VIP treatment and helped Donna with decisions. I basically slept much of the time, went out for meals, and gave approval to the various choices made -- sometimes with the attitude "Whatever you decide, dear, is fine with me as I probably am not going to be around much longer." To which her reply was "Well, just in case you are, what do you think?" When we left in two days, Donna had made all the decisions about our new home and my mother and Hiltje knew of our situation.

I had applied for disability status with the Social Security System and had a couple of interviews. As was the case with most new applicants, it was denied. Donna wanted to stay through Reformation Sunday in October because she related to a group of teenagers who were due to be confirmed. The next day (November 1) we signed over the papers to the new owner of our condo and we were off to Florida. We had our furniture and belongings loaded up by a mover who was very reasonable. We stopped in Waterloo, Iowa, where Hiltje was, and were at The

Villages on November 4. We had the walk-through in our new home led by our agent the next day. We had closed by mail so did not see the house until that day. On the November 6 the movers arrived.

We settled into what has become the home we have lived in longer than any other: 1307 Santa Rosa Court.

Healing

Our dear friends, Bob and Bonnie Weisenburger, who had traveled with us to India, offered to organize a healing service for us. Sunday afternoon, March 21, was set at Our Redeemer Lutheran Church. John Weisenburger, who had made the decision to be a pastor when he was in Africa with us, and his wife, Lori, provided the music; Bob and Bonnie worked with one of their pastors, Dick Beckman, a member of the Order of St. Luke, a cross denominational organization that promoted healing primarily in Episcopal circles. I had experiences with healing services in the past and felt that they should have a place in parish ministry. We announced it just days before. There were those who came who were curious and didn't know if Lutherans should be doing this. But there were several, especially pastor friends, who believed like I did that healing should be part of the offerings of a congregation.

Avoiding the sensational and tying the service to scripture, Dick Beckman appropriately took attention away from him and pointed to the gospel. He spoke directly to me and I was touched. When it came time for the laying on of hands and people were invited to participate, we were flooded with people. With Donna close by and some 15 pastors participating, including all of those from the "Cassette Group," I was overwhelmed by their caring, but even more important, I was relieved of the pain and anxiety I felt. Dick Beckman prayed that I might let go of it all. Sobbing and with all those hands on me, I released my spirit and was filled with the Holy Spirit like the rush of a mighty wind. There is no doubt in my mind that healing had taken place! That reality was confirmed in the weeks that lay ahead.

Donna was relieved of the pain she had felt and had a very uplifting time leading a workshop in Rochester. Doctors were not only amazed that I went through such an ordeal and was still alive, but MRIs and CT scans showed a steady improvement. They revealed that healing was taking place and that, while there was still a false lumen (an additional channel of blood in the abdominal area), all the organs were being fed. They knew that something different had happened. I could only praise God for this miracle of healing. There is a sense that each day since has been filled with God's grace. I am deeply and humbly grateful.

Since that time I have had a yearly MRI which, when placed over the one of the previous year, is the same. In Florida I was placed under the care of Dr. Robert Safford, head cardiologist and chief of medical staff at the Mayo Clinic in Jacksonville, Florida. He has remained my main doctor for all the time I have been in Florida and has become a true friend.

Golfing

Ever since I started golfing as a caddy, playing golf has always been a part of my life. I played almost daily during the season of competitive golf in high school and college, in spurts overseas, and while getting settled back in the States. After settling into parish ministry, regular golf was possible and I embraced it.

Sometime in the early 80s I joined Oak Glen Golf Club in Stillwater. Through Donna, I had reconnected with an old golf buddy, Emery Barrette, someone I played with on the Hamline team. Over the summer months when things slowed down in the parish a bit, I was able to get out on the links. Emery introduced me to Howie Schultz, former NBA and MLB player. Howie was a Hamline Piper and one of those rare athletes who had played two major league sports, baseball for the Brooklyn Dodgers and basketball for the Minneapolis Lakers. He was a natural athlete. The first time I played with him he sank a putt on the first hole that was at least 60 feet long, went through the fringe of the green, and came back to the hole. Both he and Emery were residents of Oak Glen. Hamline had an annual tournament, which I chaired one year. Oak Glen also had competitions. Bob Sander and I won at the annual member-guest event one year. Midweek and Saturday competitions provided a great time and we flighted so that the competition was always fair at a similar level.

When I hit 50, I was eligible for the team in the "Minnesota Seniors League." This league had about a dozen different clubs around the Twin Cities and a weekly match that included eight players from each team. We played scratch golf, that is, scores were always in relationship to par. The first five scores were posted and matched with players of all the teams. It was competitive, but great fun. Howie and Emery also played.

In July of 1992 we received a phone call from the daughter of Emery, who had terminal cancer. "Dad has this dream of playing at St. Andrews in Scotland. We would like to make it possible for him to go." They needed someone who played golf, who knew Emery and Audrey, and traveled. We were the first ones they thought of. Of course we said yes. Using our terrific travel agent, Kathryn Leslie, and frequent flyer tickets, we were off to Scotland inside of three weeks between chemo treatments. Emery was weak and I did not know if he would make it. But he gained strength as we went along. We played Royal Troon, Turnberry and Glenn Eagles (all British Open sites) and the day we played St. Andrews was a glorious day with the sun shinning. Emery appeared in knickers dressed in traditional garb. When we returned, Emery had gained strength. He died the following spring. We were delighted that we could be a part of making his dream come true.

Life in The Villages

When we first arrived at our new home, there was the excitement and challenge of getting settled into new surroundings and getting to know friends in the neighborhood. Norm and Carol Berg came down to help us settle in. Donna has a knack for getting to know people. Her outgoing personality and gift of gab are a great asset. We were just the ninth household to move into our "Villa de Laguna," a small sub-unit of just 51 homes in the middle of a golf course. We became a fairly close-knit community during those days. We came from various places up north. People hailed from Minnesota to Massachusetts and had a variety of employment prior to retirement.

We got together with the neighbors socially during those first years. A weekly golf group went out, we had gatherings for special events in the spring and autumn and at Christmas time. We were all in the same boat, new to the state and finding out just how things were done here. It would be years before Donna and I would call Florida "home." This in part was due to the fact that for several years we traveled back and forth. Our family ties were in Minnesota, and there were events that we wanted to be a part of. But Donna also had her consulting business, and I was involved at Luther Seminary with the Global Mission Institute.

Summers in Florida were hot, so we tried to journey north during that time. While I was at GMI, we had missionary housing nearby, utilizing vacant quarters and bouncing from one to another of the units. We had a car that we left. We also stayed with friends and family. During several summers we stayed at a rustic cabin in Wisconsin, owned by friends, Shirley and Dan Sorenson. Of course, we had several persons from the north visit us during the winter months.

The Villages is a growing, dynamic community, unique in its concept and philosophy. It is sometimes referred to as "The Disneyland for Seniors." When we moved in, there were 7,000 residents. In 2008 there were 70,000. With good advertising, activities galore, (there are well over 250 golf holes of every caliber, a thousand activities each week, classes for all, and live entertainment), there was plenty for everyone. At first it was more affordable for us, but it has become less so in recent years. But it as everything you can think of for seniors: hospital, wellness center, recreation centers, bowling alleys, swimming pools, movie theaters, shopping and much more! A golf cart community, residents use the golf cart as a second car.

We live just 50 miles from Disney World, Sea World, Universal Studios and other attractions. The airport (shuttle service provided) in

Orlando is also about 50 miles. Traffic becomes very congested during the winter months when all sorts of "snowbirds" abound.

As time has gone by, with health problems and rising gas prices, we have stayed in Florida all summer. Golf is cheaper here and life is more relaxed, but it is hot during the summer. It reminds me of how it was in Malaysia.

Return to Painting

Fine art has always tweaked my interest, but for many years I could not pursue that interest with production, having devoted time and effort to vocation. As I moved close to 50 years of age, I realized that if I was ever going to paint, I had better get started. So I started taking a painting class at the community college. In the process I connected with an old friend, Ray Rossbach. We exchanged paintings and talked of old times.

While I could not devote a lot of time to it, it whetted my appetite again. I branched out and took classes from a Chinese artist in St. Paul. I focused on semi-impressionistic landscapes in a popular style. When we moved to The Villages in 1993, I took up painting seriously. I joined the local arts association, then several in the area, and began taking workshops. The talent that God had given quickly became apparent. I have always viewed the beauty of God's creation with a sense of awe and gratitude. Much of what I paint is an extension of that appreciation coupled with the belief that any talent I might have in art is a gift from God to be used so that others might also see the beauty of life. Painting is a spiritual experience, a divine encounter of media, a God-given idea and a person's ability to create. So as I paint I try to get in touch with my inner spirit and find there more ideas and inspiration than one can paint in a short lifespan.

It was an incredibly creative time in my life. I would wake up in the middle of the night with an idea. I would get dressed and rush to the garage (turned into a studio), eager to put my thoughts into a work of art.

Frequently it was on a special type of cold press paper that withstood the rigors of multiple layers of paint and the work of various tools I would use to create. Tubes and bottles of various colors of acrylic paint would splash on the surface as I would work, often working on three or four pieces at once. I was eager to see what would emerge as I used a process that was itself creative. And when a work that brought it all together would emerge, I gave thanks to God for the inspiration and the opportunity to be involved.

This went on for several years. As my Parkinson's advanced and as I was freed up to express my thoughts, my work became increasingly abstract. Sometimes I was disappointed, but usually surprised when a pleasing composition would appear. I received affirmation by artists whom I respected and by judges who would award prizes at shows.

Duain in conversation with Doug and Carol Watnemo
and Gordy Lundberg at art show at Luther Seminary 2007

I enjoyed learning new techniques and styles. I tried to transfer my feelings in a variety of ways, thus the variety of media. I enjoyed each one and worked toward having sufficient expertise to best communicate what I feel. Though I was not confined to one style, I focused first on acrylics and found the challenge of layered acrylics exciting. It was something that was different and brought out my love of color and bold strokes.

As I layered the paint and made designs from various funky tools, there was always that "aha" moment when a creative idea took an unexpected and unplanned turn. I started to do semiabstract work and then delved into the abstract. I continued to have a plethora of creative ideas, which confused or excited my colleagues, but left me with a sense that God was in control and not me.

As time went on, I have been awarded ribbons in a number of shows over the past 11 years. I got to know some of the artists from the area and learned from them. After a couple of years, I was diagnosed with Parkinson's Disease, but for many years carried on my art work, becoming more abstract, and depending more and more on the spirit to guide my strokes. It was amazing what God can do. I became very productive and in a couple of years I produced over 200 paintings per year. Plus I again took up ceramics. But as time progressed and my PD advanced, it was more difficult to produce.

Mike Daley volunteered to set up a web site that has helped in getting my art known. The Villages and central Florida, however, are not a Mecca for abstract art. I think it was one year when I made a concerted effort, I actually had more income than expenditures from my art. But it has been enjoyable and I am blessed by having the experience and associations that have come as a result of my art. I paint little now, but still am active in the arts community.

I have been privileged to have a number of my paintings sold and hang in homes. Others hang at institutions. Each I pray is a tribute to God. I have had shows in The Villages, Tavares, Mt. Dora, Ocala, and Minnesota.

One is never sure what impact a given painting will have. One recipient described how a painting interacted with her pain and struggle. She concluded: "I am convinced God used your painting, Duain, to further unfold the power of Christ's life, death, and resurrection. How could you have known, when you were painting it, all the ways God would reveal Christ to others?" She's right, of course, and I am just so thankful that God has used my painting in some small way to get through to others.

Hope Lutheran Church in The Villages

Settling in at The Villages, we began looking for a local church. We had a relationship with several Episcopalians who were worshiping at the newly built Church on the Square and attended worship there occasionally. St. John was a small church in rural Marion County that had a good feeling but lacked the kind of leadership that we felt was important to the growth of the community. We eventually joined Gloria Dei Lutheran Church in Leesburg even though it was about eight miles away. Pastor Kemp was a good preacher and seemed to have a good understanding of the church. I helped out at both churches, but we never really felt totally comfortable in either. Donna commented, "I want a church right here in The Villages."

As things in Minnesota began to wind down for us, we increasingly turned our attention to Florida. I attended the annual assembly of the Florida-Bahamas Synod of the ELCA, where I pursued the thought of starting a mission congregation in The Villages. It seemed to us like the ideal spot and demographics for the start of a new congregation. The bishop referred me to the mission director, who promptly brushed me aside with the comment: "Oh there are lots of places like that in Florida; we can't possibly start a mission at all of them." The next year when I approached him, he seemed only slightly more interested.

In the meantime, others were working on the same idea. Tom Langevin and his wife, Pearl, were speaking to the former bishop, Lavern Franzen, who happened to be married to Tom's sister. Tom was the former president of Capitol University and ran a business that employed interim presidents at universities. They were members of St. John Lutheran Church in Marion County and had also been trying to get the mission ball rolling. We united forces and were finally able to get a commitment from the synod to explore possibilities. A group of people from St. John and Gloria Dei met with Kathy Baines, the bishop's assistant on November 20. We decided to proceed immediately and hold a public meeting of interested persons. On December 2 over 100 persons attended a meeting. Rev. Ron Ryckman, Synod Mission Director, indicated that he had the green light to proceed.

We met with the developer, who was open to the idea and identified a centrally located site at the intersection of Morse Boulevard and Highway 466 in Sumter County. Tom and I continued to take our dog and pony show to the news media (The Villages has its own newspaper and TV station). A second interest meeting was held in March, when it was confirmed that a Pastor Mission Developer would be called.

In June, the Langevins, Donna, and I met with a candidate for our mission developer, the Rev. Barry Hunteman. We discussed our vision for mission in the new congregation. I felt very strongly that mission outreach should be our focus from the beginning. Barry Hunteman concurred and indicated that he would welcome such an emphasis. I had observed that a congregation that exists for others is a growing congregation. We talked about the theology of mission and the place of the pastor. Barry received the call.

Those first days were filled with excitement and anticipation. Barry used our home for his headquarters the first few months, so we got in on the ground level of starting a mission congregation. Donna facilitated a meeting of members to name the congregation utilizing a group process she had previously used. When the decision had been made, she turned over the paper bearing the name to Barry, who then announced, "Hope Lutheran Church has been born."

The newly birthed mission congregation purchased 6.44 acres of land in The Villages and was therefore eligible to receive special favors in acquiring space for worship. Our first worship service was held at La Hacienda Center with 203 worshipers in attendance on Reformation Sunday, October 25, 1998. At that time there were 18,000 residents in this growing community. We were a church on the move and like the ancient tabernacle pulled up stakes as we traveled about. We began growing almost immediately, eventually outgrowing three rooms at La

Hacienda and moving on to the large room where public events took place at Savannah Center.

After just over a year of worship, we officially organized with 335 charter members. By that time we had paid off the $325,000 loan for the land, came off mission status on January 1, 2000, and called Pastor Hunteman. We got somewhat sidetracked in our mission with a multimillion dollar building project. As The Villages grew, so did the church. Without a whole lot of effort, numbers soared to over 1,500 by the end of 2008.

As pastoral staff was needed (up until 2009), Pastor Barry decided to use several of the retired member-pastors, the idea being that they could focus on what they enjoy the most in ministry and supplement their income with a part-time position. I resisted this for some years as I felt that the work I did should be voluntary. For some reason Pastor Hunteman felt threatened by me, and there was an obvious tension in our relationship. He did end up hiring me for over a year in the area of mission outreach. It needed attention and is always struggling to be on firm footing. Barry has changed with the times, adjusting structures as he has gone along. He is a popular preacher. I believe that the church continues to exist in spite of us, and to the degree that it is focused on mission, it will be accordingly blessed. Because of demands on space, we have attempted to start a second campus without success. We currently are considering a plan to enlarge available space where we are. A second full-time pastor was hired in June 2009. During "the season" when snowbirds come, our worship attendance swells to about 1,300 with Easter drawing well over 2,000. With weekly attendance on average of about a thousand, we are considered by some to be a "mega church."

When we started the church we knew it would grow rapidly because the demographics. Donna and I give thanks to God that we were able to contribute in a small way.

Mission at Hope

As it is the tendency of congregations in a community like The Villages to focus on themselves, we knew that mission would be a concern of few. All the more important then that we get off to a good start and lead the way for others.

Within the Mission Outreach Team we have a plethora of activity. Recently, we increased our involvement with Resurrection House, connected to the Farm Workers' Ministry in Tommy Town near Dade City. This is a cross-cultural ministry focusing on children that is close to The Villages and appreciated by a growing number of Hope members. New opportunities have been established with Slovakia and Albania. In April of 2009 we sent 10 people to Martin and Nitra, Slovakia, and one to Ecuador on a medical mission.

Addressing a crowd in Ranchi, India, 2007

India

Our most active overseas involvement has been with the Northwest Gossner Lutheran Church located in the Ranchi area. This is directly related to Nijhar Minz and her coming to Luther Seminary while I was there. I had visited with her people on a trip to India in 1986. Nirmal Minz, Nijhar's father, is one the great saints of the church and the former bishop. After Nijhar married, she and husband, Neeraj, came to the States and we had some engaging conversations. We discussed his vision for the church in India. It seems his church was left out of the loop when it came to international ecclesiastical contacts due to a shunning created by past actions. Neeraj and Nijhar shared with great passion their desire to serve and assist with establishing a school of theology there. The more I spoke with them, the more I shared their vision. They began to collect funds toward a building for a multi-training center. Even though they would not be returning to India for a couple of years, they were able to excite people. I took that excitement to Florida with me and shared it with St. John (who had never had a mission project before) and with people at Hope. It was marvelous to see the Holy Spirit at work in the various people.

They encouraged us to go and establish contact with the church in India. Donna and I made a trip to the Northwest Gossner Lutheran Church in 2004. When we left the States, I had in mind three important things to address. First, there was the role of the Ekka family. Second was approval to proceed with building a modest center in which pastors, evangelists, missionaries, and lay leaders could be trained. Third, and important for the church, was connecting them with international agencies, thus gaining the church some recognition so that they would not be left behind.

We started out in Madras with a visit to Gurukul, a Lutheran theological school. This was important to share with them our vision and to announce our intention to get involved. Before we left the States, I had been in conversation with the Ekkas and the World Mission Prayer League, a pan Lutheran movement and mission agency that the Ekkas had discussions with in terms of their work. I was able, by the grace of God, to get the leadership to invite WMPL to visit. This took place just days after we left. I was able to email Chuck Lindquist, director of WMPL, and arrange for the visit. This opened up a whole set of new relationships for the Gossner Church.

While in Ranchi, we received a firm commitment of their intention to proceed with the training center. We had a prayer of dedication at the site for the center, and we had a clear understanding that the Ekkas would have a key role. Mission accomplished! I was ecstatic over this progress. We enjoyed our time with the people and learning from them. They have the marvelous custom of washing the feet or hands of guests and dancing at every occasion. Their main offering is rice that the women bring to church and dump into a bin. It is brought forward for the offering and afterwards sold, with the income going to the church.

We returned in 2007 along with dignitaries from WMPL, and by then the Ekkas were also there. By then my Parkinson's was becoming quite advanced, but I was able to manage. It was an added blessing to have friend Carol Khong with us from Malaysia.

While serving on the Global Mission Committee of the Florida-Bahamas Synod for a few years until I was faced with health problems, I had the responsibility of relating to the Evangelisha Lutheran Kirch in Suriname. A small church with only a few congregations, it dates from 1741 and was the first Lutheran Church in South America. I enjoyed speaking Dutch again when visiting Suriname. Our synod support has primarily been for a new ministry in a suburb of Paramaribo. Hope Lutheran now supports the new missionary, Kevin Jacobson, in his ministry of training the laity there.

It was fulfilling to have the connection with local people in a foreign culture again, even though I could not complete my responsibility there. I also visited Guyana twice.

Other Activities

Each Epiphany season Hope focuses a special emphasis on some aspect of mission. Speakers visit from our various national missions department and the World Mission Prayer League. The Ekka family and the president of Luther Seminary, who is a missiologist, were also here. We had programs lasting several days that highlighted the Middle East. After 9/11 Roland Miller came, spoke on Islam, and led several workshops. The principal of the Bible School in Martin, Slovakia, came with his family in January 2010, We have also had several mission festivals (some which included other churches).

In an effort to keep mission before the congregation, our main bulletin board is devoted to mission, and occasionally other bulletin boards as well. We're trying to grow. We recently had a retreat that was helpful. I have also taught mission courses. One is entitled "What's Happening in Mission?" and ran for four weeks during Lent. Donna heads up the local "Seeds of Hope" fund-raising campaign for the Wildwood Soup Kitchen and Food Pantry.

We figure we are so blessed that the least we can do is help those who are hurting and in need of a word of grace.

14. PARKINSON'S

In the summer of 2000 I noticed tremors in my right hand. These got worse in the months ahead. By the time we got to the Malaysia Missionary Reunion in Arizona in October, I was having difficulty controlling my right hand. It continued to get worse as the months went on. In January 2001 the doctors at the Mayo Clinic in Jacksonville officially gave the diagnosis, confirming what I had suspected for some time. I had Parkinson's disease.

I was familiar with the symptoms as my father had Parkinson's for nearly 40 years. He was one of the first in Minnesota to go on L-dopa, an early form of the main drug that has been used for years in treatment. This gave Dad at least a dozen additional years, and he fought a brave battle before succumbing to it at age 84. In the end he was bedridden, unable to talk and having difficulty swallowing. There is still speculation about the cause of Parkinson's and studies abound. There is hope that a cure may be found but, in spite of much speculation, so far it has not happened.

Part of being able to cope with Parkinson's has been my familiarity with the disease through my father. There has been a steady, but not rapid, advance of symptoms over the years, particularly of tremors on the right side of my body. By 2007 it was a definite hindrance. I had difficulty holding anything in my right hand. I continued to be as active as possible, golfing and doing Tai Chi, but by midyear it was obvious that, if possible, something needed to be done. During my good times with medication, I was able to function fairly well. I managed to shoot my age, an even par 72, on our local championship course.

Miracle 2

Not many people get to face death squarely and walk away from it, praising God. I have been privileged to do it, not once, but twice. The first was a dissecting aortic aneurysm that forced me to retire. The second was the result of an infection. It happened in St. Luke's Hospital then used by the Mayo Clinic in Jacksonville, Florida, just after we had returned from our journey to Asia in December 2007. We had set up the date of December 13 for Deep Brain Stimulation surgery for my Parkinson's, with the follow-up surgery a week later. When I went in for pre-op on December 7 the surgeon was positive and said it should be a "slam dunk" operation. I had the special apparatus put on my head and all was set for me to be awake throughout the two-hour operation. However, when he placed the stimulator into the thalamus, the results (tested by my mechanical responses) were not what he had hoped for. Asking me if I was willing to have a second implant, which he recommended, I gave an affirmative reply. I did not know, however, that it would take an additional two and a half hours of surgery and numerous probes to implant the second stimulator into the sub-thalamus. After four and a half hours of brain surgery requiring that I be awake the whole time, I was able to rest.

When I awoke, it was not a pretty sight. The left side of my face had become severely swollen. It would get worse. I went home to recover, but there were too many side effects from the surgery. Fortunately, Donna picked up on them and documented them. When we met the surgeon on December 18, the second (follow-up) surgery was scheduled for later that day, but in light of the swelling inside the brain, a disjointed thought process, loss of words, it was cancelled. Steroids were prescribed, which helped for a few days, but by December 22 I had difficulty walking and was losing speech, disoriented, and had a fever of 103. I was rushed to the hospital in Ocala by ambulance. When stabilized, I was sent by ambulance to St. Luke's Hospital (Mayo Clinic) in Jacksonville. On

December 27 I was discharged since the fever was gone and walking had improved. The following day I returned to The Villages.

I was restless, having speech problems, unsteady on my feet, disoriented, and agitated. The fever started to go up. Donna called the Mayo Clinic. They recommended bringing me back as soon as possible. I have no recollection of the next several days. Donna drove me up to Mayo Clinic in record time. At the emergency room I was severely disorientated and combative. I was fighting for my life. Restraints were put in place. A lumbar puncture showed a severe infection. My fever spiked at 105. Antibiotics were administered in time to save me. Donna had been told that when I arrived, I had only a few hours to live. All I could move for several days were my eyes.

On December 30 I was diagnosed with surgical bacterial meningitis of the gram-negative family. I was assigned four main teams of doctors: Internal Medicine, Infectious Disease, Neurology, and Neurosurgery. An entry into "CaringBridge," an online service made available to families of patients needing to communicate with family and friends, read: "Duain showed his fighting spirit to the doctors."

It was during this crucial time that a very special angel came to us to help. She is Rachael Khong, daughter of our dear friends in Malaysia, Peter and Carol Khong. Rachael offered to help and she arrived just as Donna was taking me back to the hospital on December 28. She stayed with Donna and me during that first crucial week in the hospital when life hung in the balance. There was so much that needed to be done. Rachael was the one who got us onto CaringBridge and made regular entries in the first month. Even after she returned to her home in Springfield, Missouri, she continued to phone Donna each day. She took copious notes and reproduced them so that thousands of people could be kept apprised of what was happening. Rachael is a Christian and her faith comes through in the text of what she wrote, referring to me affectionately as "Uncle Duain." A gifted writer with obvious computer skills, her caring spirit came to all who have plugged in.

Rachael started daily reports while I was in the hospital, and continued from Missouri while I was in the nursing home. I quote from one of the many stories she told, this dated January 8, 2008, 08:03 pm CST:

Hi guys,

. . . I want to mention that God has truly put all these amazing people together that have rallied and supported Auntie Donna and Uncle Duain through the good times and especially during the bad times. The hospitality that I received from their friends when I was there was gracious, genuine and heartfelt.

The flashes of Uncle Duain that we do see are what to cling on to and continue believing. To be still and know that God has it all under control. Today Uncle Duain again wanted to wait for everyone to get there before he started eating and those moments where he reaches out for a hug, smiles, or says I love you both with his voice and his eyes....those are the moments where I know that my Uncle Duain is still there and will come back eventually.

It's a long road but I know just as well as Auntie Donna that we're all sticking around for the journey. Thank you all.

hugs and blessings,
racheal

Then from an entry of January 15:

It is going to be an interesting transition but I have faith that things will go well, and if anything, Philippians 4:13 says that I can do all things through Christ who strengthens me. In this case, it is with the kind people that God has put in place to help tie up all the pieces together.

So I guess the prayer requests for tonight would be for God to continue the healing in Uncle Duain and to continue lifting Uncle Duain and Auntie Donna in His loving arms. To ask that God will bless this transition, that it will run smoothly and to know that He is there guiding them along and carrying them.

Thank you again for reading, we appreciate you.

hugs and blessings,
racheal

It was a joy and privilege to officiate at Rachael's wedding in March, 2008 in New Orleans (even though I was weak and still without the second surgery).

My time at the nursing home was interesting. Donna had a couple of uphill battles to fight with staff. One was because they had apparently lost a part of my med list, and consequently I was not being medicated properly. Then, failing to read the report of me, they had proceeded to list me as having "dementia." Donna was my constant advocate with staff, and facilitated a lot of progress. I was placed in a room with a man who had diabetes, had the habit of keeping the TV on all night at a loud volume, entertained people long into the night, and talked on the phone late as well. Needless to say, I did not rest well there. Other than that, we got along well and she tolerated my mistakes in identifying various objects, my frequent packing, and missed wording and timing. For a month beginning in the hospital, I was put on IV antibiotic, which required a dedicated person to come in the middle of the night. The main person with this responsibility was a man with military experience. It was like an angel appeared in the dark of night, gently woke me, and placed the IV in me. About 45 minutes later he came and removed the IV, saluted me, and quietly left. It was for me an eerie experience, but I appreciated very much his commitment and care.

I was up very early and waiting for others to start their routine. I had rehab classes in speech and general conditioning each weekday. I was able to show some of the staff my art website, though I could not handle the basics of the computer. I did a few Tai Chi moves. The staff was good to me. The speech therapist was helpful. When I first saw her, I could not relate objects, had difficulty finding words, and were so soft spoken that people could not hear me.

There were several persons who participated in my care during those days of hospitalization and nursing home care in Jacksonville. Hiltje and Dane each spent about a week. Dane took the nightshift when I was in the hospital, providing round-the-clock care. He would then go to the Hampton Inn when Donna and Rachael returned from an evening of rest, sleeping during the day. The staff at the Inn was very supportive of Donna during her long stay. Paul and Mary Vierow, cousins who reside in The Villages, provided transport of persons to and from airport, delivery of items from The Villages, sitting, and generally doing whatever needed to be done. Jan Gold, Bill and Sue Ann Corkish, Valery Plummer and Ron and JJ Frambach all played a supportive role.

I was released on January 22. Dr Yu asked me to recite John 3:16, which I did, adding 3:17. I left with an overall sense of God's continued grace in my life and with gratitude for Donna. Although I was weak, had lost hearing, and could not express myself well, the improvement was sufficient.

We were overwhelmed by the sheer numbers and caring of church related people once we returned home. We had been on the prayer chain and our progress was announced each week at services. Donna knew that she would need a lot of help when we returned, so she requested that those interested in providing care and sitting while Donna did errands sign up. She got a grand list of persons, male and female, who were willing to volunteer their services. She got such a long list that she could not use everyone who was willing. She also took over the journaling on Caring Bridge.

On January 28 Donna wrote:

With Racheal as my coach, I (Donna) am writing in the journal tonight. Words cannot express my gratitude to Racheal. I feel she has been my special angel, sent by God to lighten my burden and provide a process for support and prayers during these challenging days.

I want to thank you all for your prayers and support. After long days in the hospital and at the Rehab Center it was comforting to know we had so many friends around the world praying for us. Thank you from the bottom of my heart.

We have been home a week now and I want to share with you how Duain is doing and progressing. He has been evaluated by Home Health Nurses and therapists - speech, occupational and physical. The doctors at Mayo Clinic are still saying that he will regain everything but his hearing of high frequency sounds. We are researching hearing aids.

Duain looks good. Everyone who sees him is amazed. His color is good. His hips are weak and he is a bit unsteady. He likes to walk. He has lost 25-30 pounds. He has a good appetite and is on a normal diet.

The occupational therapist is helping him with adapting to life with tremors in his right hand and arm. She has experience with Parkinson's patients and some with patients who have Deep Brain Stimulators. She sees things very positively and Duain finds her helpful. Our goal is for the stimulators to be connected and that the tremors will be gone. Right now the tremors are "out of proportion" as they were prior to the surgery.

Duain's work with the speech therapist is most challenging due to swelling in the brain from the surgery. Duain is finding more words and his memory is improving each day. He experiences difficulty with basic orientation, some comprehension and numerical concepts. His attention span is increasing and he is working really hard in this area. It is frustrating for him because he knows that he knew these things. Our challenge is in not pushing too hard and praying that the doctors are right in saying it will all come back within a couple of months.

Duain is enjoying visits by our church family who stop by during my errand time and appointments, although he does not think it is necessary to always have someone in the house with him. His lumbar puncture is now scheduled for 12:00 noon on February 19 (his second surgery was postponed until April 21) at The Mayo Clinic in Jacksonville. Please continue praying that the infection is clear and that plans can be made for the second part of the surgery.

Duain is showing interest in mission activities at our church, Hope Lutheran, and in art. He is still finding the computer and remote controls challenging, but is making more attempts.

We praise God for Duain's healing and many blessings. We thank God for your friendship in Christ. Duain's helpmate – Donna :)

Thanks to Racheal, I guess this does work. You are a good teacher!

Over the next six weeks we were helped by people offering to do whatever they could. Fortunately, Donna had the skills to orchestrate it all. The main thing was relieving Donna so that she could have time for herself and run errands. These people all knew me from church. They would usually bring me a treat of some sort, be prepared to take notes, and went walking with me. All of them were very pleasant. Some brought over delicious meals for us as well. I was in rehab with home health care folk each day and had certain exercises to do. One person went home early since I saw no need for him to stay. That was a no no as I was to have someone with me at all times. When I walked, I was usually tilting to one side.

Donna, ever the cheerleader, reported in March:

Praise God! Wow what a week! Duain is off and running. By Sunday the headaches from the spinal tap were significantly reduced, Duain headed for the golf range to hit a few balls. He was back home and tired within 20 minutes. On Monday he went out and hit a few more and said it felt better this time. He has not yet played a short nine, but he is thinking about it. Our weather became cold and windy so he felt it best to put that activity on hold.

Tuesday Duain's hearing aids came in and he is trying to get used to them. Wednesday he commented that the fuzziness in his head was gone. He thought that the hearing aids helped. Even when he takes the hearing aids off his head feels better. I am thinking that there has been another reduction in swelling of his brain. Whatever caused this improved feeling in his head, it is good.

Duain is REALLY feeling independent today. He drove the car again for the first time since December 12. A friend took him out for a test drive. They reported to me that they saw no reason why he could not drive and everything had gone very well. Tonight he drove me to a fund-raiser for 'Seeds of Hope' at Chick-fil-A. It felt like a date. I had been thinking that he was ready to drive again. It was good to have the idea of driving independently supported.

The neurosurgeon was right. He said that the more Duain does the faster things will come back. Duain will be out golfing as soon as we have a warmer day. I can see his strength improving daily as well as his ability to find words. His memory is definitely improving. He is looking good.

Healing is such a wonderful gift. Many, many prayers have been answered. Thanks be to God.

Love to all, Donna

Finally by the first of May my vocabulary and writing skills came back to the degree that I was able to communicate the following, dated Friday, May 2:

"Give thanks unto the Lord your God, for He is good; for His steadfast love endures forever." Psalm 106:1

As I look back over the past 19 weeks I cannot help but give praise to God for His steadfast love. Even those weeks that I was totally out, in a coma or close to it, God's love was ever present. And when I was told I had just 12 hours to live in December, He was there too. Once again I was spared for a reason. You may recall that when I had two feet of dissected aortic aneurysm back in 1993 and was not expected to live, I experienced God's healing and was able to serve for several years in ministry, in the arts, and in establishing a congregation. Now I ask myself "What does He have in mind for the next several years?" I would be interested in your response to that question.

For one thing there has been an outpouring of God's love through the congregation at Hope Lutheran Church. I was placed on prayer lists galore, with thousands praying for me each day. I cannot thank these people (indeed, many of them remain unknown to me), but I would like to thank as many as possible and share with you my story. Please, if you know of others that were involved, pass this letter on to them.

Having just returned from an exciting trip to Malaysia and India, we continued with my planned deep brain stimulation (DBS) surgery at Mayo Clinic/St. Luke's Hospital on December 13. The rest of the story you can read on the web.

Thanks be to God for all of you. His steadfast love does endure forever! I am overwhelmed by your caring.
Duain (Sonny) Vierow

On Tuesday, May 6, Donna wrote:

Dear friends,

We spent this a.m. at the Mayo Clinic. Duain's right hand was steady so there were no adjustments on the stimulators. The stitches behind his ear were removed. A return visit was scheduled for July 21. If needed we can call and return any time. In the meantime we have work to do.

Duain can drive again and play golf as tolerated. He was strongly encouraged to get back to exercise - walking and tai chi. First, he will reduce one medication and maybe go off it within two weeks. Then start speech, occupational, and physical therapy. He plans to do one therapy at a time.

Duain feels that he has a new lease on life. We stopped at the Nursing Home - - South Point Terrace where Duain resided for therapy for more than two weeks. The staff was thrilled to see him. He is a perfect example of just what therapy can do. The visit gave them a boost. The daughter of one of the speech therapists wrote a report on Duain. She needed to write a school (elementary) report on a local artist - - she chose her mom's friend. She has been following Duain's art website. It was a good day. We praise God. The miracles continue.

Love. Donna

I have worked at rehabilitation the last two years, and was able to recover some of my basic abilities. Countless numbers of persons have been involved. Their encouragement and prayer is an inspiration to me. I continue to help out at church in a limited capacity. I have been able to recover sufficiently to officiate at a wedding of the relative in Spokane and to enter art shows again, receiving an award. I'm back to playing golf and have lowered my expectations on results.. And I am doing some writing on the computer.

A Parkinson's support group is a part of my regular schedule. I have found them to be a helpful and caring group. It is amazing how well they manage in spite of their disabilities and of how supportive they are for the effort put forward. The Villages has a terrific program of resource persons, classes and opportunities for people with PD. We do special exercise for persons with PD. There are speakers with expertise and a weekly "Fight Parkinson's" exercise group that is encouraging. While I cannot function and participate as I used to, I find life a joy as well as a challenge. I am grateful for all the support I receive. A second PD group has an informative monthly meeting.

Fifty Years of Ordination

In May 2010 I celebrated the 50th anniversary of my ordination with two open houses, one at Hope Lutheran Church in the Villages and the second at St. Mark's Lutheran Church in North St. Paul. They were grand affairs organized by Donna and assisted by people from the mission team at Hope and friends in St. Paul. Attendance represented people from my various involvements in The Villages and classmates, 4-Hers, former congregation members, and friends in St. Paul area.

Donna has a friend, Jim Reitz, who put together a DVD which summarized my life and ministry, featured Dane speaking on being a missionary kid and made an appeal for giving to the newly established scholarship for international students at Luther Seminary. I was honored when the Council at Hope voted to establish the scholarship in my name. All funds brought in at the celebrations were contributed toward this fund. People have been very generous in giving.

15. SHEER GRACE

Summary Reflections

"The gifts and the calling of God are irrevocable." Romans 11:29

From the days that I spent with the "Sons for the Ministry" program, I believe that God had a plan for my life. The question was whether or not I follow it. When I prayerfully considered this and yielded my spirit to God, it was clear the path I should take. As the years pass, I was affirmed in the decision to become a pastor, but God had a further call for me. That was to be a cross-cultural missionary of the Gospel.

Truth of the matter is that I have always felt my primary call was as a cross-cultural missionary. The call to ordained ministry has always been a part of that, but it has been incomplete without the second call. There is no greater call than to be an ambassador of the Gospel of our Lord. To do that cross-culturally is the ultimate call and challenge. When I yielded to God's will, I experienced a tremendous freedom and affirmation.

For 50 years, I have been fascinated by the challenge to explore the many factors that play into obtaining the most complete data possible in analyzing cultures and their receptivity to the Gospel. I then developed a strategy that would best speak to the specific people, given the fact that they are on a journey that is ever changing, trying always to keep the integrity of the culture and the authenticity of the Gospel.

Over the years I have been blessed with insights that have made a difference in how and what is communicated. The work of the Holy Spirit is essential to this process, as is prayer. And God has led me at key times in my life to have an impact on what has been done in the name of Christ. One such occasion was in our visit to Ranchi, India, in 2004, another was the development of the Global Mission Institute, and still another was in Malaysia in our approach to Tamil Indians.

In a way it was unfortunate that I got sidetracked from that calling while I did parish ministry in Minnesota. But it seemed that I had no other choice at the time as I was facing the divorce and needed to stay stateside for the children. I do not regret having made that choice. But I do regret the fact that I was forced to make it.

In a sense I was a victim of my own inadequacies. I am, in the end, like all of us, a sinner in need of grace.

It is true that I did keep my missionary vocation alive through my continued involvements beyond the local parish (synod service, GMI, international travel). These aspects of ministry and their importance to me were not adequately understood.

It would have been interesting to see how I fared as a teacher. I certainly had much growth to do in that area. The brief encounters with teaching I enjoyed (Gustavus Adolphus College, lay training in Malaysia, Luther Seminary) especially the subject matter and students, but not always the structures that went with them.

Sheer Grace

Life has been an incredible journey. When one looks back over the events of my life, one has to conclude that I have been incredibly lucky or richly blessed by a loving God. I know it to be the latter for I have found at each stage of life that when I acknowledged and sought God's will, there was clearly a sense of divine guidance. It has been a journey of faith, for one cannot comprehend or deal with all the challenges one faces alone. But in our weakness, grace abounds. I am reminded of Paul's words in II Corinthians 12:9 "My grace is sufficient for you, my power is made perfect in weakness. So I will boast all the more gladly of my weaknesses, so that the power of Christ may dwell in me." I know that in my weakness there is strength. In my weakness somehow God's power miraculously dwells within me. I hope that the underlying message of these memories have been reflections on a life filled with the grace of God. As I look back and forward, I am touched by the sheer grace of God in my life. To deny that would be a mistake of major proportions.

Grace was and is evident throughout my life, most dramatically perhaps during the two miracles of healing that have brought me to this day. Through these two events God has spoken to me and others of a grace that knows no bounds. This grace cannot be contained nor explained by human activity or words. I am sorry that I cannot adequately express the feeling of gratitude and inner joy that I have. God's grace is amazing, indeed. The past two decades of my life I have found comfort in Romans 12:12: "Be joyful in hope, patient in affliction and faithful in prayer."

Grace sustained me and came through many others. I had the gift of a caring family and community, of supportive classmates, teachers, and colleagues.

Grace came through persons that were part of 4-H Club work and youth ministry (Luther League). These two organizations helped form my character and leadership skills during a crucial time.

Grace has come through the church. The call to ordination and the call to be a missionary came through the church and key persons along the way represented a grace-filled God as they ministered to me.

Grace was perhaps most dramatically felt as I worked with my brothers and sisters overseas. For it is in the missionary life that I experienced the testing of faith and the acceptance of God like none other. The education I have received along the way was filled with God's grace.

Grace has been evident through the great crowd of witnesses that have surrounded me over the years. Caring, concerned, and praying people have made a profound difference.

Grace has come to me through two lovely children, Hiltje and Dane, constant reminders of God's activity. I have been further blessed with five lovely grandchildren.

Grace has been evident to me in the actions and love of Donna. She represents to me the daily grace that I have been so blessed to know. She has embraced my passions in life and helped me reach my dreams. Our trust level is high.

The hand of a gracious God: sometimes stirring the pot; sometimes giving me a nudge; sometimes revealing, dramatically, his will; but always with a caring love for me that enabled me to serve Him throughout my life.

This story is, ultimately, not about me. It is about the grace of God. All my life I have experienced it and I can only say, gratefully . . . thanks be to God . . . for manifesting such amazing grace to me.

RELEVANT DOCUMENTS
BY DUAIN VIEROW

Published Materials

Devotionals:
The Home Altar, Jan., Feb., March 1970, Jan. 15-28
The Word in Season, Vol. 41 No. 3 Entire Issue,
    with illustrations.
The Word in Season, Easter-Pentecost, l972, May 14-27
The Home Altar, July-Sept.1972, Sept. 17-22
The Home Altar, July-Aug. 1974, July 1-7
The Home Altar, Oct.-Dec. 1975, Dec. 22-31
On the Move with the Master (A daily devotional Guide
    in World Mission), William Carey Library, 1977
The Word in Season, Epiphany-Lent, l981, March 9-22
The Word in Season, Pentecost, 1983, July 4-10

Articles:
The Lutheran, March 16, 1966, "Mr. Ambrose Builds a Chapel,"
    pp. 18-20, with photos
The Lutheran, March 29, 1967, "Swedish Missionary Elected
Bishop by the Church in India" p. 34
Lutheran Women, Jan. 1971, "The Skies Are Friendly, But...,"
    pp.10-13

Response, June, l971, "The Skies Are Friendly, But… ,"
pp. 28, 29 & 50

Lutheran Women, Apr. 1972, "Building on Roots in Selangor."
pp. 12-15

World Encounter, Spring 1972, "Lake Andrew on Fire for Mission,"
p. 35

World Encounter, Feb. 1974, "Upgrading Without Degrading,"
pp.14-16

World Encounter, Fall 1974, "A Young Church Reaches Out,"
pp. 8-9

World Encounter, Summer 1978, "How I See Our Global Ministry,"
an interview, pp. 10-13

Learning With, March 1979, "You Can Help Make Mission
Education Happen," pp. 13 & 14

Ytblick: Svenska Kyrkans Missionstiidning, June, 1970,
"Vad Gjorde Vi For Felt, pp. 6, 7 & 17.

Eva – Het Ruk Der Vrouw, "Zij Verlegden Hun Horizon,"
21 Sept., 1957, pp. 32-33.

Books

"Chinese Lutherans in Peninsular Malaysia: A Case Study" in
Christ – The Church's One Foundation, The Lutheran
Church in Malaysia and Singapore, 2010, pp.22-32

Cross Roads of World Mission, booklet and leader's guide,
Parish Life Press, Philadephia, 1981, booklet - 64 pages,
Leaders Guide - 22 pages.

A History of Lutheranism in Western Malaysia and Singapore,
Board of World Missions, 1968

"The Status of Global Mission Structures," in Mission at the Dawn of the 21st Century: A Vision for the Church, Paul Varo Martinson, ed., Kirk House Publishers, 1999, pp. 268-290

"Tamil Lutherans in Malaysia West," in Church Growth in the Third World Roger E. Hedlund, ed., Gospel Literature Service, 1977, pp. 283-337

Edited: Malaysia Christian Handbook. 1979 Glad Sounds

Edited: "Movements in the Church," a journal of the ALMS Theological Conference for Laity and Clergy, 1980. Published by The Affiliation of Lutheran Movements

Unpublished materials:

"Theological Training in a Malaysian Setting – a Draft Analysis", 57 mimeographed pages, May, 1974

"A Comparison of Tamil and Chinese Lutheran Churches in Peninsular Malaysia and Singapore," unpublished dissertation for Doctor of Missiology degree at The School of World Mission, Fuller Theological Seminary, 266 pages, 1976

"The Tiger, the Pigs and the Elephant." A children's story with illustrations, 1968

"Devotionals by Duain," Advent 1981, Christ the Servant Lutheran Church

"Gift of Daily Devotionals" to members of Our Redeemer Lutheran Church, 1990

"Christian Evangelism Among Indians – A Survey" (mimeographed) 1974

Report on a Visit to Sumatra (mimeographed) 1967

"The West Malaysian Churches and 'Dynamic Equivalent' Forms" (mimeographed) 1975

Malaysian Church Growth News (for the Malaysian Church Growth Committee) 1973-75

"Synopsis of a Year's Discussion on Theological Training" (mimeographed) 1976.